MONEY FOR JAM

The Essential Guide to Starting Your Own Small Food Business

Oonagh Monahan

OAK·TREE·PRESS

Published by OAK TREE PRESS, 19 Rutland Street, Cork, Ireland

www.oaktreepress.com

A catalogue record of this book is available from the British Library.

ISBN 978 1 78119 090 6 (paperback)
ISBN 978 1 78119 091 3 (ePub)
ISBN 978 1 78119 092 0 (Kindle)

Cover design: Kieran O'Connor Design
Cover illustration: lepas2004 / iStockPhoto.com
Author photo: Frances Muldoon Photography

CONTENTS

ACKNOWLEDGEMENTS

When I told people that I was writing this book, their reaction, almost without exception, was extremely positive and encouraging. The wonderful food producers that I have enjoyed working with so much have been very generous in providing me with their logos and information to use. Food producers are some of the most hardworking people I have ever met – there is nothing easy about the food business; there is no getting away from the long hours of work; they'll never make a fortune; and despite that, they continue because they love what they do ... most of the time!

Thanks to Birgitta and Peter Curtin of the Burren Smokehouse; Siobhán and Paul Lawless of The Foods of Athenry; Simon and Lindy O'Hara of Coopershill Venison; Margaret Farrelly and Roberto Macias Escutia of Clonarn Clover; Sharon Sweeney of Cannaboe Confectionery; Rosaria Pisieri of Algaran; Tom Butler and Michelle Costello at Cuinneog; Eamonn Lonergan at Knockanore Cheese; Declan and Mary T. Molloy of Molloy's Artisan Bakery/Honest; Detta McNiffe of McNiffe's Bakery; Simon and Siobhán Stenson of Cherry Blossom Bakery; Geraldine Mulgrew of Parkview Farm Duck Eggs; Margaret and Brian Phelan from Glenfin Farm; Bernie Quinn Duck Eggs; Jane Cassidy of Kilbeg Dairies; Paul and Carmel Williams, The Irish Pasty People; Paul O'Malley of Jack & Eddie's Sausages, Andrew Pelham Burn of Carrowholly Cheese; Sean Casey of Westport Grove; Redmond Cabot of Red's Sauces; Úna Martin of Úna's Pies; Anthony Creswell of Ummera Smokehouse; and Kieran Murphy of Murphy's Ice Cream.

Thank you to Eileen Kelly, Amanda McCloat and Dr. Elaine Mooney of St. Angela's College in Sligo for their direction and technical verification. Thanks are also due to Jim Fitzsimons of Riverwest Management for allowing me to reproduce information from some reports I prepared for him previously. Lastly here, thank you to Barry Murphy of Pure Sales for the marketing information in **Chapter 7**.

Also thank you to Meabh Conaghan of Enterprise Ireland and to Bord Bia for their advice about outsourcing production and protecting your idea.

I have gathered the information used in *Money for Jam* over many years, so if I have forgotten to acknowledge or thank anyone, please accept my apologies for the omission.

Finally, enormous thanks to my great friends and family – my mother, Ann, for fostering my love of food (smoked cod pizza anyone?) and most especially my husband, Frank Quinn, and my children, Emmet and Anna – for their support, patience and encouragement. What's for dinner?

Oonagh Monahan
Dromahair, Co. Leitrim
September 2013

1

INTRODUCING THE OPPORTUNITY

Have you ever thought about trying to earn some money from producing food? Are you the person everyone goes to for their lemon meringue pies, apple tarts and other desserts for family occasions, christenings, first communions or other events? Do you have a garden of rhubarb or other fruit? Do you make jam every year and give it away when you could be selling it? Do you fancy the idea of making cheese or yogurt or ice cream but don't know where to start?

If so, then this is the book for you – it will tell you everything you need to know or show you where to find it for yourself. *Money for Jam* is structured and written in an easy-to-follow and easy-to-read format. It is not a textbook – think of it instead as your trusty companion, more of a handbook or manual. It aims to reassure both prospective and current early-stage food producers. So don't be intimidated!

Money for Jam contains everything that someone who is new to the food business will need to get started and to keep going. It will help bakers, jam and honey-makers, ice cream, yogurt and cheese-makers, egg producers, sausage roll, pie and pasty-bakers, chocolatiers, and dessert-makers.

It covers the what, where, who and how for small food producers – including legislation and registration, labelling and packaging, suppliers and distributors. This is the part that puts off most would-be small-scale food producers. The complaint I hear all the time is that people don't even know where to start or who to ask for information in relation to starting a food business. Many are afraid to stick their head above the parapet by asking the Environmental Health Officers

(EHOs) at the Health Service Executive (HSE), the Food Safety Authority of Ireland (FSAI), Bord Bia or the other development agencies. There is a common perception that doing so may bring unwanted attention – or worse, inspection! But EHOs and the agencies are there to protect the consumer *and* to help you as a producer.

Consumer Trends

Bord Bia is great for all sorts of industry reports. Among them is the 2010 *Consumer Attitudes to Local Food*, which says that, as a result of the boom that Ireland experienced since 2000, consumers like the idea of Irish people doing well now – the entrepreneur is valued. As a result, we hear people talk about "wanting to support their own".

On the other hand, once the boom times ended, nostalgia for simpler times became apparent – people harked back to when life was perhaps less complicated. Part of this is that people say they want simpler food ... and simple food means meat, vegetables and soup, homemade and wholesome.

The past 10 years have seen a huge change in the way people think about the food they eat. Gone are the days of limited choice, low quality and tradition. People are now used to having a wide choice. People talk about food in ways they never did before. Standards have increased and with them, so have people's expectations of quality, value and availability.

The average person now knows their organic from their locally-grown, and their air miles from their sustainable. Not alone that, but with cheap air travel and the influx of other nationalities into Ireland, the consumer now wants to try out new foods. What was exotic some years ago is run of the mill now. My mother reckons she didn't taste broccoli until she was 30! It just goes to show you that the foods many of us consider to be part of our basic shopping basket today were considered exotic and unusual years ago. And the same thing will happen in the future for foods that are considered exotic or unusual now.

And, more than ever before, shoppers are really interested in knowing where the food products they purchase are made. In addition, consumers care about health and nutrition, ethics, quality, naturalness, craft, and story and heritage. So, their decision to buy a food more often than not will depend on whether that particular food meets these concerns.

Some small shops have responded well to this demand for quality and choice from customers. A typical example is a small butcher in a country town, who might sell bags of potatoes and some vegetables, might have packets of spices on the counter, even might offer the occasional apple tart. The same butcher has now re-branded themselves from *O'Leary's Butchers* to *O'Leary's Fine Foods and Delicatessen*. The shop has had a facelift, it's a bit more attractive inside and the layout has been tidied up. They are still selling the same foods but they have raised the bar in terms of how the consumer sees them. As a result, they are attracting new customers, offering an outlet and showing support to local producers who want to sell locally, and demonstrating that they are on board with the whole 'foodie' culture that has grown in Ireland in the past 10 years or so.

Opportunities for Small Food Producers

But what does all this mean for you, the would-be food producer? For a start, if you have been baking, or making jam at home, more or less as a hobby, perhaps the pressure is on now to make some money out of it either to add to the household income or with the ambition to grow it into a decent business that will earn you a living.

Consumers like the idea of supporting their own, as I've said. They want to see money staying in the country, preferably locally. So, locally-made produce is very much welcomed and can be seen in shops everywhere.

Consumers also like the idea of artisan or hand-made foods. While that may not always be the reality, it is important to maintain that image for your customers. Like the Tardis in Dr. Who (small on the outside, enormous on the inside), you might portray the image of a country kitchen making scones and jam, while all the time backed up by a state-of-the-art food production unit in your converted garage!

The boom was not all bad, despite what you might think! While the crash has been hard for many, Ireland's consumers are more experienced now – they are used to having a selection of foods to choose from, they expect good quality; and they are used to paying for it, even if the frequency of purchase might not be quite what it used to be. Farmers' markets and country markets have become the norm for many shoppers, not just some quaint novelty. Consumers will still make a special trip for special purchases that they cannot get in supermarkets.

The Artisan Food Market

Teagasc has reported that the production of speciality food in Ireland accounts for approx. €500m *pa* from a base of about 300 producers. Artisan/speciality food production in Ireland is made up of a large number of small food producers. The sector comprises niche products generally made in small batches, using artisan techniques.

It is generally acknowledged that the artisan/speciality food sector is growing and is an important part of Ireland's food industry and so to the economy. Small speciality and artisan food producers' sales are growing by an annual average rate of 12 to 17% according to the TASTE Council's 2006 *Submission on Better Business Regulation for the Artisan/Speciality Food Sector*, which shows the growing market demand for artisan and speciality food (the TASTE Council is a voluntary representative group of the smaller food business sector made up largely of local, artisan and speciality food producers).

The key point of all of this is that, if your products are good quality, made in Ireland, consistent, have great taste and flavour and ideally provide something a little different, then there is probably a market for them.

What Does 'Artisan' Mean?

One word that is over-used these days (apart from 'passion'!) is 'artisan'. As a result, its meaning has become diluted. In a report for

Bord Bia, the TASTE Council found that, while the term 'artisan' is associated with hand-crafted, home-made or small-batch products, it does not necessarily guarantee good quality. John McKenna of the *Bridgestone Guides* has his own definition, which he calls the Four Ps. Artisan food encompasses: **person; place; product; and passion.**

The combination of artisan and a high level of craftsmanship does result in superior foods. For the consumer, main understanding of the meaning of artisan is the connection to the producer themselves – the actual person who makes the food. In the consumer's mind, this means home-made or hand-made.

So artisan means superior taste, flavour, hand-made, small-scale, direct connection to the producer, high standards – and so more expensive? The important point is that consumers like artisan foods: they like the idea that someone has made this food themselves, that it's not some big, faceless, corporate, automated process. They like it, but are they are willing to pay for it? The difficulty faced by artisan producers is that they are in competition with those very same big, faceless, corporate, automated processors that can make and sell their foods much more cheaply. It's not so much that artisan foods are dear; it's that other foods, because of mass production, have become relatively cheap.

Thus the artisan producer has a job to do in promoting all the qualities of their foods that justify the price – back to flavour, quality, provenance, authenticity, person, home-made, farmhouse, local, Irish and so on. Those are your potential unique selling points (USPs) – more about them in **Chapter 2** – and you must never underestimate their value or forget them.

'Local' Is Important

When you think about 'local', do you think about your corner shop, village, town, county, province or country? When is local not local? And if you think in a particular way, then you can be sure that the people you intend to sell your food to also will think the same way. After all, until now, you have been just a consumer too (of course, once you've read this book, you'll be all set to become a food producer yourself!).

For some people, local food means that it comes from literally a local farmer, butcher, baker or a neighbour. There is most certainly a trend among consumers towards supporting local producers and shopping locally to keep the local economy going. If your name or the name of your food or business does not immediately tell the shopper that the food is Irish or made locally, then you need to make sure that you let them know some other way (more about this in **Chapter 7**, when we look at branding).

The small food business has potential for several reasons:

- Consumers have an expectation of being offered a variety of foods;
- There is a consumer population with the ability and willingness to discern and to pay for high-quality locally-produced food;
- Increased education and awareness levels of farmers and producers;
- Increased popularity of locally-produced, home-made and farmhouse products;
- An image of Ireland as an unspoilt leisure destination that is green, natural and wholesome;
- Increased number of new entrants to the food sector;
- Availability of high-quality and high-profile local cuisine in the form of well-known, local artisan food producers across the country, thus raising the profile for all producers.

If someone goes to the trouble to look for Irish or locally-made food, then they usually have a good reason to do so. Most of the time they want to support local producers and be sure that their food can be traced back to where it was made. The phrase 'farm to fork' is used commonly now, and it's all about traceability – knowing where food and its ingredients come from and being confident as a consumer that you can trust that information. You can use your labels and branding to help communicate this message, and more about that later.

So, when is Irish not Irish?

- If it's made in Ireland? Even if the company is not Irish-owned?

- If it's not made in Ireland, but the company is Irish-owned?
- If the basic ingredients are not grown in Ireland, yet the food is made here by an Irish company?
- If the name implies that it's Irish?

Or is it just a matter of opinion? What do these logos tell you?

The average consumer usually doesn't know enough about the food industry and neither reads nor understands product labels enough to be able to work their meaning and to decide whether a product is Irish.

So there is a great opportunity for you to shout about the fact that your foods are made in Ireland, by you, in your kitchen, employing local staff (even if it is just you and your family), using Irish ingredients ... or a combination of some or all of these.

The Advantages of Small Food Businesses

As far as the shopper and consumer are concerned, the main advantages of small food businesses are that the food is locally-produced, that it has low food miles as well as a low carbon footprint perhaps, is sold locally, that there is a story behind it that they can identify with (the 'provenance'), but most of all, that the food has superior quality and taste. It can have all the local, eco, history and whatever you're having yourself in terms of information, but if it doesn't have great quality and taste, then no one will buy it again. This leads to a key point about developing your food idea – **make sure you get the taste and quality right first** before you start telling everyone how great it is!

Irish food has the reputation of having high standards, good quality and trustworthiness. Food producers and suppliers should never forget the value and importance of building their brand around the provenance of their produce. Consumers like the idea that the food they buy is artisan, home-made, almost made for them especially. They like to get information about the producers themselves, the farm, the family, the recipe being handed down through generations, tradition, history of the herd or breed and so on. It helps the consumer to satisfy themselves that the food is local, has not been overly-processed and meets their expectations of taste and quality. So where to start?

2

STARTING OUT

Don't be paralysed by fear! Starting your own small food business is not like splitting the atom or finding the cure for a terminal disease. It's just cake, jam, whatever! Plenty of other people are already doing it, so it cannot be that difficult, right? It's a piece of cake! Right?

Nonetheless, there are so many different things to consider when starting up a food business that it can seem overwhelming. First things first, then.

What Will You Make?

Bread, buns, muffins, cupcakes, jam, cheese, confectionary, desserts, drinks, pies, eggs, micro beers, smoked foods, yogurt, salads, dips, chutney, fruit coulis, soup – it's your choice.

Before you do anything else, you must make up your mind about what food you want to produce. Many small food producers get into the food business because they love making a particular type of food. Others get into it because they see a business opportunity in a niche area. Many new producers try to do too many varieties and become overwhelmed trying to manage them all. Some decide to produce foods that they really don't enjoy making but do so because they think there is a market. Others do not have the skills required to make the food they think they would like to sell.

It is easier to make what you know already. Go with your strengths. If you don't enjoy making it, you'll not stick at it. So the first thing is to tell yourself that you are now in business, selling food for money. It may be just a few buns, tarts or whatever first – just in one shop or market to begin with. But take baby steps, and when your confidence builds, then start to walk with your foods to a few more shops ... jog to shops in the next town ... run, grow the business if that's what you want to do ... but all in good time.

Lots of new producers get all excited about their venture, which is great. I love enthusiastic people. However, sometimes the excitement focuses on the fun stuff: branding, packaging design, thinking about growth in the future, nationwide sales ... before they ever develop their food. All brand and no product. So first, you have to make something.

Where Do Ideas Come From?

For many people, getting into the small food business is a matter of looking differently at what they might be doing already. You might make desserts on request for family and friends already and now want to sell them ... to strangers. Perhaps it's a case of trying a new venture simply because you've always wanted to give it a try. Or maybe you've lost your job (or your husband/wife/partner has) and it's a case of having to do something to bring in some money.

Whatever the reason for it, now you need to get your thinking cap on and decide what it is that you want to produce:

- Have you spotted a gap in the market? *I can't get good gluten-free bread anywhere!*
- What are you good at? *People love my lemon meringue pie/brown bread!*
- Do you already have a source of ingredients? *We have loads of rhubarb in the garden ... I could make jam, pies, chutney!*
- What are the market trends? *I tasted this great food when we were away in Spain.*

You also need to consider who will buy your wonderful foods. More about your customers, who they are, what they want and when they eat in **Chapter 6**.

Who Are Your Customers?

Your potential customers fall into two groups – the general buying public (the consumer) and the shops who will buy from you to sell on to their customers. Both groups look for the same things: quality, taste, value and something new. Consumer trends are such that consumers are more discerning now, are used to having a wide range of foods to choose from, and are aware of organic, local and sustainable foods.

Your target market of consumers is made up of consumers of different types. Think about who they are. Are they families, older people, children, single people, married couples, men, women, healthy eaters, dieters, indulgers, students or workers? Your target market will influence the size of portion you make: large or small, multi-pack or single pack? Your portion size in turn will influence your selling price. Next, consider your packaging: pre-packed or unwrapped? If your food is aimed at the on-the-go market, then portion size and packaging style both need to be considered. There is more about all of this in **Chapter 5** on Product Development.

Retailers are also your potential customers, since unless you can sell to them you may not reach the consumer at all. Many retailers are keen to promote Irish producers; they want to offer their own customers a choice and to introduce new lines to bring in more trade. They know that the consumer prefers to buy Irish when they can, so the retailer will see your food as a way of meeting that demand. What you must remember, though, is that the retailer will not want more of the same – so try to offer something different.

When approaching retailers, be prepared! Practise your spiel first, be clear as to what your USP is (more of that below). Also, work out your costs so you know what wriggle room you have when it comes to negotiating prices. However, many smaller shops will be happy to try your foods out on a sale or return basis to begin with. In other words, they don't buy them from you, but take a cut on whatever is sold, and you take back whatever is unsold. The retailers are in business after all.

Who Are Your Competitors?

If you go into almost any small village shop, there will be at least two varieties of most foods. Take apple tarts, for example – your competitor might be another small home baker in the locality, or a large bakery delivering to the same shop, or the shop's own in-store bakery. Most shopkeepers like to offer their customers a choice, so they provide a range for the shopper to choose from. Competitors also include anyone selling rhubarb or other fruit tarts that might distract your potential buyer away from buying your apple tart. So your competitors include the cupcake lady, the Swiss roll man, as well as the large supermarkets, the discount stores ... and the list goes on.

Everyone and every product has a competitor, whether it is an obvious one or not. So don't fool yourself that you have no competitors. It's just not the case. Realising that and acknowledging it is really important when it comes to promoting and selling your foods.

You should benchmark yourself and your food against your competitors. What are they doing well that you might emulate? Can you beat them at their own game? What can you offer that is better than the food that is available in the shops?

What Is a USP?

A unique selling point (USP) is a characteristic or attribute that distinguishes your foods from your competitors. Identifying and promoting your food's USP is an on-going task. You can't just say it once and sit back waiting for either the customers or the money (or both) to pour in! You will need to remind your customers about it all the time.

Some examples of a USP include fancy packaging, sugar-free, yeast-free, gluten-free, no preservatives or additives, low-fat, home-made, locally-produced, organic, uses local ingredients, or a new type of food product, new to this country, new to this area, healthy, different portion sizes, you name it! Whatever the USP is, you must be clear about it in your own head first, and then be able to talk about it and promote it all the time.

A USP defines your food's competitive advantage. It is essential to identify what makes *Oonagh's Apple Pie* different from its competitors.

Who Should You Talk to First?

If you go to the Food Safety Authority of Ireland (FSAI) website (**www.fsai.ie**), you will find a downloadable leaflet telling you that the first thing you should do is acquaint yourself with the relevant legislation. For most people, that's enough to send them running for the hills. Legislation? NO, thank you!

However, if you're in this game, then there is no avoiding the legislation. The important thing is to know what applies to you and what does not. There is the challenge – how do you find this out? And, once you know what applies to you, then how do you interpret it?

Depending on the foods you want to produce, then your kitchen might be either very straightforward to organise (bread, cakes, jam) or not be suitable at all (meats, prepared salads, large amounts of anything). If you are going to make anything at home, or even if you plan to convert your garage or move into a small premises, then the very first thing you must do is to phone your local Environmental Health Officer (EHO) at the Health Services Executive (HSE). EHOs are the people who will give you approval for producing anything at home in most cases.

If you are planning to get into hen or duck egg production, or animal slaughter and handling and/or processing meat, or making dairy products, then it is the local Department of Agriculture, Food and the Marine (DAFM) office that you should contact. Your local authority also may inspect establishments involved in animal slaughter and handling and/or processing meat, making dairy products or producing eggs also. So check out your local authority website or call them to find out who you need to talk to.

We will look in more detail in **Chapter 3** at food safety and hygiene.

Thinking Things Through

For the best chances of success, you will need to think through all of the issues that affect how you will make, where you will make and how you will package and label your food. In addition to your job as production manager, you also most likely will be the financial controller, sales and marketing manager, administrator, trainer, staff supervisor (if you have any one working with you), delivery van driver, and chief bottle washer too!

It is very difficult keeping on top of everything, of that there is no doubt. Your chances of success will improve if you at least know all the things you are supposed to remember. Make a list (keeping everything in your head is impossible) and if you can't do it all yourself, then get some help.

Many women in particular who have started up a small food business from home still try to maintain their other 'job' as housekeeper, parent, cleaner and cook. You need to acknowledge the fact that you have now set up a business. It might be at home but it is still a business. Schedule time for when you will be 'at work' and during that time, no other household chores should distract you. Easier said than done I know, but you must aspire to achieving that goal ultimately.

Common Reasons for Failure ... and How to Avoid Them!

Food products fail all the time – usually for one or more of these reasons:

- **Poor market research among consumers or retailers or poor market orientation (in other words, trying to sell to the wrong people):** You thought your product was great, your family and friends told you so, and maybe it was. But none of the customers wanted it. Or you didn't target the right customers, or there was already a well-established or even a better version already on the market and it was impossible to convert shoppers to buying yours;
- **Technical problems:** Product problems or defects in production. Perhaps making a few cakes in your kitchen was manageable, but

once you started making 100 every week, it just couldn't be done at
home due to limitations with your mixer, oven, and/or
refrigerator. Or, while your recipe worked well for a 6″ cake, it
didn't rise when you tried to scale it up for a 12″ cake. In this case,
you needed to do some recipe tweaking (or product development,
in other words). When using common ingredients in a new way or
in a new product, knowledge about the effects of consuming
volumes greater than usual might affect how the food behaves –
for example, pears are good for treating constipation, but is this an
effect you want from your product?

- **Insufficient market effort:** An assumption that the product will
sell itself. One of the jobs that some food producers hate is having
to get out there and sell. Most will be happiest in the kitchen, up to
their arms in flour or sauce. However, if you don't or can't do it
yourself, then get someone who will and who will do a good job
representing you and your product and will make sales. We will
look at how best to approach this in **Chapter 5**;

- **Bad timing:** Nothing as obvious as trying to sell Christmas cakes in
July, but perhaps the market wasn't ready for your chilli chocolate
bars/low calorie stout/kidney bean brownies. Indeed, it may be
something you could not have anticipated, such as a local factory
closing down thereby reducing people's income, the result being
that they are not willing to spend money on indulgences such as
cakes/hummus/dips;

- **Higher costs than anticipated:** If sales and marketing is one
bugbear, then financial planning and costs analysis is the other for
most food producers. Everyone hates looking at the figures. You
must calculate how much it costs you to make, pack, distribute and
sell the food. You must do this sooner rather than later. If you don't
do it, then you cannot put a price on your products except by
taking a wild guess. If at the end of the year, you have worked
every hour of every day and sold hundreds of pots or pies but still
have no money for shoes, then there is a problem. We will look at
how best to approach this in **Chapter 8**.

In order to increase your chances of success, learn from the experience of others:

- Produce to consumer demand for the artisan/premium market;
- Get the training you need – don't presume you know it all;
- Develop online sales later, perhaps for foods that can be shipped easily;
- Use your network of friends, neighbours, family and colleagues – it's great for spreading the word and for exchanging information;
- Promote your USPs and brand values – quality, flavour, taste, provenance;
- Build awareness about your brand and your food by telling people about them all the time – word of mouth, advertising and so on **(Chapter 6)**;
- Develop new markets over time – always be on the lookout for opportunities, don't get complacent, you never know who will come in on your turf;
- Keep your product range fresh by bringing in seasonal and occasional varieties, try new packaging or labels.

In order to maximise your chances of success, you must control the things you can control. You must find out the things you don't know. Knowledge is power. After that, you are at the mercy of the marketplace, the economy, and the unknown unknowns!

Just Do It!

If you don't become paralysed by fear, then you might be overwhelmed at the thought of trying to manage everything. However, most people don't go from zero to huge volumes overnight. It is most likely that your success will grow slowly at a steady pace.

There is a bigger danger that you might plan and plan and plan, but never actually make anything. My advice is to "Just do it!". Get on with it! Make a couple of loaves/pots/jars and get yourself down to your corner shop and see whether they'll take them from you. What's the worst that can happen?

3

NAVIGATING THE FOOD LEGISLATION MINEFIELD

Before you even begin to tackle food hygiene, let's take a look at who is responsible for the legislation and for monitoring that it's being done right by food businesses (cafés, restaurants, hotels, food producers – and you!).

Legislation and Monitoring

The Food Safety Authority of Ireland (FSAI) is the government-appointed authority dedicated to protecting public health and consumer interests in the area of food safety and hygiene. Its principal function is to take all reasonable steps to ensure that food produced, distributed or marketed in the State meets the highest standards of food safety and hygiene reasonably available and to ensure that food complies with legal requirements, or where appropriate with recognised codes of good practice.

FSAI has the primary responsibility for controlling the safety of food. It delegates some of its functions (inspections, for example) to other bodies such as the Health Service Executive (HSE) and the Department of Agriculture, Food and the Marine (DAFM), but it retains the final responsibility.

FSAI is responsible for the enforcement of all food legislation in Ireland. It does this through the HSE (Environmental Health Officers – EHOs), DAFM, County and City Councils, Sea Fisheries Protection Authority (SFPA) and other bodies. Which one of these applies to you and your food business depends entirely on what you are making:

- For most people producing small quantities of food at home, it's the EHOs in the HSE. The EHOs' job is to ensure that food legislation is followed properly. They are also educators and advisors and they work very closely with the owners of food businesses to build compliance with the law. The EHO ensures that you, as a food producer, understand that there is a law, what your obligations are under that law and what the possible consequences might be if you do not comply;

- DAFM is responsible for anyone processing milk or making dairy products. Anyone who wishes to manufacture a dairy product or process milk for direct human consumption must contact the Dairy Hygiene Division within DAFM in the first instance. An information pack is issued to the potential producer, outlining what is involved in the approval/registration process, the relevant application form(s), copies of the relevant legislation, FSAI *Guidebook for New Artisan Producers,* Milk Quota FAQ (this only applies to cows' milk), TB Control Plan (goats' milk only), and a list of suppliers (goats' milk and also raw cows' milk).

While all of this might sound a little frightening, be assured that the FSAI, DAFM and the EHOs are there to help you.

You need to contact your local EHO (find contact details on **www.hse.ie**) and let them know that you have just started or are about to start up. The concern that people most often voice to me is that they are afraid that the EHO will close them down and stop them continuing. There is only one answer to that – you must make sure you keep your EHO on-side!

To keep them on-side, contact them sooner rather than later. They will visit your home kitchen and take a look at your set-up. They will tell you whether your home kitchen is suitable or not (and you may be surprised to find that you have little or no work to do to get it up to scratch!). They will offer you great advice about what changes you might have to make.

Your EHO is your best advisor – they are the ones you must satisfy. And if you don't register with them (in other words, let them know you're in business), they will catch up with you eventually.

Whether it's from spotting your jam/tarts for sale in shops, seeing your foods at markets or shows, seeing your adverts or just hearing about you, they will find you.

FSAI has a great website: **www.fsai.ie**. It also publishes a *Safe Catering Pack*, with a DVD, which you can buy and which has all the documentation you need. FSAI's *Business Start-up Packs* (cost €65), each targeting a particular food business sector, include:

- Information about the steps required to be taken when setting up a food business;
- A copy of the relevant food hygiene legislation;
- A copy of the appropriate Irish Standard published by the National Standards Authority of Ireland;
- FSAI *Guides to Food Safety Training*;
- FSAI information pack on Hazard Analysis and Critical Control Point (HACCP).

Is Your Kitchen Good Enough?

In many cases, modern kitchens are well set to provide all that is needed to satisfy the EHO's requirements for kitchen production – in other words, that you can start away. You need to be able to manage what you are making in terms of not posing a health risk to anyone who eats it. You are selling to the public now, so what might be OK for you and your family at home, might not be OK for food being sold to the public.

Simple things like keeping your food business ingredients separate from your household ingredients can be achieved by buying some big lunchboxes and sticking a label on them so that other members of the household don't use them or mess with them. If you don't have a space (or money) for a second fridge, again put your refrigerated food business ingredients into separate, labelled containers – "Hands Off Mum's work ingredients" (and keep reminding yourself and your family that you're in business now!).

You'll need separate sinks for washing your hands and for washing utensils. Many modern kitchens have a little side sink between the main sink and the draining board. There you go – two sinks! – or perhaps you have a second sink in a utility room.

You can't have any laundry in your kitchen – that means no washing machine – it must be in the utility room.

The other rumour that abounds is that you need everything tiled from floor to ceiling or else stainless steel everywhere. Not true! The legislation simply calls for all surfaces to be easily cleanable. In other words, smooth, non-porous, in good repair. If your kitchen counter is made from marble or Formica or similar, then that will be fine. If you have a wooden surface, then the best thing is to use a plastic chopping board or cover it with a plastic cloth if you're going to be working directly on it.

Your windows should be kept closed unless you're happy to put flyscreens on them. Keep the dog, cat and children out while you're preparing food.

Best to remove all clutter from the area you're working in. If there are plants on the window sills, remove them while you're working in case they fall over and spill out onto your food or work surface.

If you are doing a lot of cooking that generates steam and condensation on your windows, you will need an extractor fan. Your hob or cooker hood might do the job.

It's all pretty much common sense. The bottom line is that if you're not sure, ask your EHO.

Finally, if your kitchen is approved but you find your oven is too small or your equipment is not suitable, then you might want to consider your options – see the next section. However, the solution might even be simpler than that – get up earlier in the morning. Seriously! One client of mine complained that her oven was too small and she couldn't supply to meet the demand. It turned out she only made one batch on a Sunday morning. Seems obvious I know, but sometimes even the obvious eludes us.

What If Your Kitchen Isn't Good Enough?

If you can't use your kitchen at home for some reason, whether through your own choice or if the EHO tells you it's not suitable, or if the changes you have to make to get it up to standard are too much for you to do, then what are your options?

One baker that I know started off using the kitchen in a pub that had closed down. The kitchen was perfectly serviceable and, after a good clean and the 'go ahead' from the EHO, he was in business, and the pub-owner was delighted to get some rental income. Another producer started off using a closed-down 'chipper' to make sandwiches for distribution to local schools and businesses. Someone else I know used the kitchen in a small café that was only open during the summer season – she started off there in the winter, just to get going, and then moved into bigger premises when she was up and running and had proved there was a market for her food (the proof being the fact that it was selling), and the café was due to reopen for the summer so she was on a deadline.

There are a number of food units that have been built around the country that can be rented by the hour, week or longer term. (What are still referred to as) the LEADER companies and some enterprise organisations that help start-ups have built proper food units finished to food production standard that you can rent – contact your local LEADER or enterprise company to enquire:

- The Food Hub in Drumshanbo, Co. Leitrim is a shining example. The Community Kitchen there has been a roaring success – for example, one producer comes in once a week, makes an enormous batch of soup, freezes it using the blast freezer on the premises, then has it ready for sale at the farmers markets over the next couple of days. Operational since 2004, the Food Hub provides 26,000 sq. ft. of premium food production space across 14 independent work units and the Community Kitchen is a timeshare production unit where start-up food businesses can make their foods in a fully-equipped kitchen, paying by the hour with no commitment other than to bring their own ingredients (**www.thefoodhub.com**);

- The North Tipperary Food Works in Rearcross, Newport, Co. Tipperary was developed by North Tipperary Food Enterprise Centre (Rearcross) Ltd. An old creamery building was converted

into a premium food workspace. There is a timeshare kitchen and
production units for rental. At the time of writing, the cost of rental
of the timeshare kitchen was €15 per hour + VAT
(**www.northtippfoodworks.ie**);

- In Northern Ireland, the Food Business Incubation Centre is
situated at Loughry Campus in Cookstown, Co. Tyrone. The
Centre was opened in 1998 and provides the food supply chain
with eight purpose-built food processing factory units finished to
the highest standards in two sizes, 175m^2 and 225m^2
(**www.cafre.ac.uk**);

- Nutgrove Enterprise Park, Dublin is currently (early 2013) fitting
out two high-spec food production units, each 59.45m^2 with own-
door ground floor access and parking (**www.nutgrove-
enterprisepark.ie / info@dlrceb.ie**);

- SPADE Enterprise Centre is a community-based enterprise centre
in the converted St. Paul's Church at North King Street, Dublin
(contact Susan Richardson, Centre Manager, (01) 617 4830);

- Terenure Enterprise Centre (Dublin) has 25 fully-serviced
incubator units (including three food units) ((01) 490 3237 /
mhannan@terenure-enterprise.ie);

- Moy Valley Resources IRD have clients occupying Enterprise Units
at a number of locations around Ballina, Co. Mayo, a mixture of
both food and non-food producers (**www.moyvalley.ie**);

- The Limerick Food Centre at Raheen provides food manufacturing
and processing units, access to equipment, a full research,
information and advice service, and a specialist Agribusiness and
Natural Resources Support Unit;

- Údarás na Gaeltachta has three food units in Co. Donegal and has
proposed others in Connemara;

- Meals on Wheels and other community kitchens that are not at full
capacity may be available if you enquire locally;

- Castlehill Foods has a 900 sq. ft. (84m^2) kitchen and food
production premises available to hire outside Killala, Co. Mayo
(contact Claire on (087) 652 6065);

- Kitchen Incubators Kerry is a new professional commercial kitchen facilities and equipment for rent by the hour (contact Eileen McClure on (087) 769 1136);
- Several other LEADER / Development companies and County and City Enterprise Boards also have food units; just give them a call (**www.nrn.ie** and **www.enterpriseboards.ie**).

Food Safety and Hygiene Legislation

Food safety and hygiene legislation is concerned about these four issues:

- The protection of health;
- Making sure that proper information is given (so that the consumer is properly informed);
- The prevention of fraud (horsemeat anyone?);
- Freedom of trade (throughout the EU).

The last one isn't really a concern for you, day to day – nor, hopefully, the second last!

The legislation that applies generally to small food producers are *Regulations EC 852/2004* (the Hygiene of Foodstuffs) and *EC 178/2002* (which sets out the general requirements of food law and food safety). There is also Irish legislation *S.I. 369 of 2006*, which is mostly about your responsibility as a food producer to comply with the law and about enforcement of the legislation.

If you read all the legislation, you'll possibly find yourself a little bewildered. It's a really good idea to ask someone to help you with this. If you're feeling brave, download a copy of *EC 852/2004* from **www.fsai.ie** and jump to *Annex II* to start. Go back and read the rest when you have drawn breath.

All food service providers, supermarkets and retailers require their food producers, processors and suppliers to comply with food safety legislation. In order to make sure that you address the concerns of your customers, and because it's the law, then you, as a new producer, must comply with the relevant quality and food safety regulations, and what's more, to be seen to be in compliance. This goes whether you decide to sell through shops or direct to the customer from your back door or through farmers' or country markets.

A good reference document is the *Guide to Food Law for Artisan/ Small Food Producers Starting a New Business* available for download from **www.fsai.ie**, which will direct you to all the legislation you need.

Jargon

You will find the definitions associated with food legislation in Article 2 of *EC 852/2004* and in Articles 2 and 3 of *EC 178/2002*. Here are a few:

- 'Food' (or 'foodstuff') means any substance or product, whether processed, partially processed or unprocessed, intended to be ... ingested by humans. 'Food' includes drink, chewing gum and any substance, including water, that is intentionally incorporated into the food during its manufacture, preparation or treatment. It includes bottled drinking water. (*Regulation 178/2002* also tells you what is not food!);
- 'Food law' means the laws, regulations ... governing food in general, and food safety in particular. It covers any stage of production, processing and distribution of food, and also of feed produced for, or fed to, food-producing animals;
- A 'food business' means any undertaking, whether for profit or not and whether public or private, carrying out any of the activities related to any stage of production, processing and distribution of food;
- A 'food business operator' means the persons responsible for ensuring that the requirements of food law are met within the food business under their control – that's you if you are a food producer!
- 'Food hygiene', or 'hygiene', means the measures and conditions necessary to control hazards and to ensure fitness for human consumption of a foodstuff, taking into account its intended use;

- 'Primary products' means products of primary production, including products of the soil (growing fruit or vegetables, in other words), of stock farming, of hunting and fishing;
- 'Establishment' means any unit of a food business;
- 'Competent authority' means the FSAI, HSE or DAFM;
- 'Contamination' means the presence or introduction of a hazard;
- 'Wrapping' means the placing of a foodstuff in a wrapper or container in *direct contact* with the foodstuff concerned, and the wrapper or container itself;
- 'Packaging' means the placing of one or more wrapped foodstuffs in a second container, and the latter container itself;
- 'Processing' means any action that substantially alters the initial product, including heating, smoking, curing, maturing, drying, marinating, extraction, extrusion or a combination of those processes;
- 'Unprocessed products' means foodstuffs that have not undergone processing, and includes products that have been divided, parted, severed, sliced, boned, minced, skinned, ground, cut, cleaned, trimmed, husked, milled, chilled, frozen, deep-frozen or thawed;
- 'Processed products' means foodstuffs resulting from the processing of unprocessed products. These products may contain ingredients that are necessary for their manufacture or to give them specific characteristics;
- 'HACCP' means Hazard Analysis and Critical Control Point (see later in this chapter);
- 'Unsafe food' – Article 14 of *Regulation EC 178/2002* requires that food must not be placed on the market if it is unsafe. Food shall be deemed to be unsafe if it is considered to be injurious to health or unfit for human consumption;
- 'Traceability' – food business operators must be able to identify any person from whom they have been supplied with a food, a food-producing animal, or food ingredient. You must have a system and procedures in place to manage your traceability. It's straightforward, but critical;

- "The hygiene package" is the bundle of food legislation applied since 1 January 2006, when existing legislation was revised and rationalised to introduce consistency and clarity throughout the food production chain from 'farm to fork'.

Registration

The law says that, before commencing trading, a food business operator (FBO) – that's you – must register with a competent authority – that's either with the Environmental Health office in your local HSE (**www.hse.ie** for contact details) or DAFM office. Failure to do so is an offence! Businesses that handle and/or process foods of animal origin need approval from the competent authority. Once you contact the HSE (which it will be in most cases for home-based producers), the EHO will go through the details of the approval process with you.

If you're not sure which one applies to you, just phone one of them and if it's not them, they'll direct you to the other! As I've said above, unless you're farm-based or are making cheese for example, it will usually be the EHOs that you need to talk to.

It is really a good idea to contact the EHO for advice sooner rather than later. Approval of your kitchen will take into account the kitchen layout, whether it is easy to clean, where you keep your rubbish (waste management), how you make your foods (processes), food safety (HACCP), your product range and how much you are making (volumes), for a start.

The reason the EHO considers the volume of food you make is that, while you might be able to manage small amounts now, things might get out of control and be hard or impossible to manage if you get too busy. If this busy-ness causes a risk for food safety, then you'll have to make some changes. However, cross that bridge when you come to it. (By the way, being busy because of demand is a good thing for you – it means you are selling lots!).

Traceability

Traceability is knowing who you bought what from and who you sold it on to if you're selling it to another business such as a restaurant or retailer. However, when you're selling directly to the consumer, through a farmers' market or your own shop or in a restaurant, then you don't need to know the names and addresses of all your customers!

You should keep a list of the suppliers you use regularly. The best way to look after this is have a sheet that you fill in every time you buy ingredients or packaging. You can get these sheets from **www.fsai.ie** or **www.bordbiavantage.ie** or do one up yourself.

Supplier Control

As a food producer, you should ensure that you use reliable and reputable suppliers and that the products you buy meet your own standards. One way to achieve this is for producers to have an agreed product specification with their supplier, including the temperature at which the product must be transported and delivered, the condition of packaging, the correct labelling, and so on.

If you buy poor quality ingredients or raw materials that cause a problem for you in the long run, then it is to you that the customer will complain. It is your reputation that's on the line. The customer is not interested in the fact that one of your suppliers is at fault; all they see is your name on the food that caused illness or whatever. So don't let poor standards from your suppliers result in poor standards for your foods.

In summary:

- All businesses must be able to identify their suppliers (supplier traceability);
- Businesses supplying their product *to other businesses* must be able to identify their customers (customer traceability);
- Any food that is placed on the market must be adequately labelled to ensure traceability throughout the food chain.

What Is HACCP?

When you are selling food to the general public, you must make sure that your food is safe. In other words, that it won't cause any food poisoning, that it is fit for human consumption and that it is not injurious to health. In order to show that you are in control of what you're doing, then the law (*Regulation EC 852/2004*) says that you must put in some sort of system or procedure to prove it (and if you are dealing with foods of animal origin, then you must also comply with *Regulation EC 853/2004*, which sets out specific hygiene rules for these types of products).

HACCP stands for 'Hazard Analysis and Critical Control Point' and is the most common and best-recognised procedure for food safety and hygiene. In the simplest terms, it means that you identify where something might go wrong (that could result in unsafe food) and you do something about it to prevent it from happening. You want to make sure the food is not contaminated by any bacteria or bits of hair or pieces of anything that shouldn't be in there. If it's not in the recipe, it shouldn't be in the food!

If you go to the trouble of putting procedures in place, then for goodness sake record it and get the credit for it! And if you do record it, make sure it has been done first!

Depending on the food you are producing, the EHO may or may not insist that you do formal HACCP training. Look out for courses in your area – see **Chapter 9** for more information.

HACCP prerequisites

Before implementing HACCP, basic food hygiene conditions and practices referred to as 'prerequisites' must be in place. HACCP then can be used by the business to identify steps that are critical in ensuring the preparation of safe food and which therefore need tighter control and monitoring.

Prerequisites include:

- Cleaning and sanitation (regular cleaning of premises and equipment);

- Maintenance (repairs and routine maintenance of premises and equipment);
- Personal hygiene (hand-washing);
- Pest control (vents and any external windows that open in the food preparation areas fitted with a flyscreen);
- Equipment (use equipment that can be thoroughly cleaned and taken apart if necessary);
- Premises and structure (the size of the premises – your kitchen or garage conversion! – must be enough to handle the volume of foods you are making);
- Services (a potable water supply);
- Storage, distribution and transport (storage of foods at the correct temperature, make sure raw and ready-to-eat foods are well separated);
- Waste management (removing waste frequently to prevent it becoming a source of food contamination);
- Zoning (physical separation of activities to prevent potential food contamination) – this really only applies if you are making cooked or other high risk foods.

Has All This Started to Put You Off Yet?

Don't worry, it's really not that difficult to manage all of this when you are operating on a small scale. It looks like a long list but again a lot of it is common-sense – you are just making sure that there is no dirt that bugs can grow in and that your food won't get contaminated with bacteria or something falling into it. Just make sure everything is clean and tidy, in good order, that you and anyone working with you are also clean and hygienic.

Once you have got the prerequisites sorted, then it is time to get on with looking at the 'seven principles of HACCP'. These are the steps that you take when organising your HACCP plan – get help with this from a training course or food safety advisor or your EHO/DAFM vet, or from the FSAI Start-up pack.

The steps are:

- **Identify the hazards:** If you're lucky, there might not be any hazards!
- **Determine the critical control points (CCPs):** If there is a hazard, what can you do to prevent it becoming a problem for you?
- **Establish critical limit(s):** What's your limit? It might be an upper or lower temperature, for example. Or if you are making high risk foods that need microbiological testing, then it will be the lab that will let you know what the result is;
- **Establish a system to monitor control of the CCPs:** How do you check? It might be that you use a thermometer or a temperature probe for your fridge or for checking the inside of cooked food, for example;
- **Establish the corrective action to be taken when monitoring indicates that a particular CCP is not under control:** If something goes wrong, what do you do? You might just throw it out and start again, you might turn down your fridge temperature setting, or turn up the heat on the cooker, or leave it to cook for longer depending on what it is you are checking up on;
- **Establish procedures for verification to confirm the HACCP system is working effectively:** Do some random spot checks now and then;
- **Establish documentation concerning all procedures and records appropriate to these principles and their application:** Write it all down!

HACCP Records

For HACCP to work successfully for you, records must be kept and be readily available. It is unrealistic to operate HACCP or to try to show compliance without being able to back it up by providing evidence such as written records. As with the HACCP system itself, the number of records you need will depend very much on the nature and complexity of your business. The aim should be to ensure control is maintained without generating excessive paperwork! Ask your EHO or DAFM vet for guidance.

Again, the *Safe Catering Pack* from FSAI is very handy for learning about HACCP and gives you all the forms you need to keep your records. FSAI also has a booklet, *HACCP Terminology Explained*, that you can download for free from the website (**www.fsai.ie**). Don't panic, it's not rocket science.

FSAI and Teagasc have a produced a workbook – *HACCP/Food Safety Workbook for Farmhouse Cheesemakers* – which you can request through the FSAI website also.

Low Risk and High Risk

A low risk food is one that is unlikely to be a risk to public health – in other words, cause food poisoning – usually because they are acidic (like pickle) or don't contain much water (like bread or jam) so bacteria can't grow easily. Low risk foods spoil due to their chemical composition (not microbiological activity) and usually have a 'Best Before' date. Also, if the food is going to be cooked before it is eaten, that will kill any food poisoning bacteria and so the consumer is protected. Bread, cake, buns, jam are all low risk generally.

High risk foods on the other hand are much more at risk of microbial contamination, particularly harmful bacteria called pathogens. These foods are generally refrigerated as a result, and have a 'Use By' date. Examples include raw seafood, freshly prepared salads, some meats and dairy products. The main reason these are high risk is because they may be eaten without any further cooking or processing, so if they are contaminated with food poisoning bacteria, then the consumer is at risk.

If you have a sponge cake that you sandwich together with a fresh cream filling, it increases the risk. The sponge itself is low risk, but because the cream is a dairy product and can go off (spoilage bacteria will grow) unless it's refrigerated, then that increases the risk. When to use Best Before and Use By dates is covered in **Chapter 7**.

Conclusion

It's understandable that a new producer just starting up may find the legislation all a bit overwhelming. Don't feel you need to know the legislation inside out and have it all at your fingertips. Just know what you need for your foods.

But that's the problem! How do I know what I need for my food? Ask your EHO for advice or ask your local County or City Enterprise Board (**www.enterpriseboards.ie**) or Rural Development Company/ LEADER company (**www.nrn.ie**) to give you a food mentor (this is often a free service) – just make sure your food mentor knows the legislation. You'll get to know it all yourself well enough in good time.

4

ENSURING FOOD HYGIENE

Basic Microbiology

A micro-organism (microbe) is a creature that is invisible to the human eye and can be seen only under a microscope. A space the size of a full stop would contain millions of them. Microbes are found everywhere – in your hair, throat, nose, colon and hands; in the soil and air; on surfaces; in food, shellfish, water, vegetables, plants ... and the word used to describe this is 'ubiquitous'.

There are five types: bacteria, viruses, moulds, yeasts and fungi. Some of these microbes are useful and good for us – for example:

- Bacteria (lactobacilli) aid digestion;
- Fungi (mushrooms) are edible;
- Moulds produce antibiotics (penicillin), and are used in making cheese (Brie rind);
- Viruses are used to make vaccines and in research;
- Yeasts are used in brewing beer and baking bread.

It's the bad ones we worry about:

- Bacteria (sometimes called 'germs' or 'bugs') can cause food poisoning and thus illness;
- Fungi cause food spoilage;
- Moulds also cause food spoilage (for example, on bread or cheese);
- Viruses can cause food poisoning;
- Yeasts – too many can contaminate liquids.

Most bacteria are harmless but many are responsible for disease and infection. Harmful bacteria are known as pathogens.

Many bacteria are capable of forming spores – a protective shell that helps them to survive when food is scarce. You are probably familiar with tetanus or 'lock jaw'. Tetanus is an infection of the nervous system by the potentially deadly bacteria *Clostridium tetani*. Spores of the bacteria live in the soil. In the spore form, *C. tetani* may remain inactive in the soil, as if it is hibernating, but it can remain infectious for more than 40 years. So that's why if you get soil in a cut, you need to wash it out straight away, just in case.

What Do Bacteria Need to Grow?

Bacteria need six things to grow:

- **Time:** Bacteria divide in half (and thus multiply) every 20 minutes under the right conditions;
- **Warmth:** The best temperature for them to grow is 37°C, body temperature, but they can grow in temperatures anywhere from 5°C to 63°C, known as the 'danger zone';
- **Oxygen:** For some bacteria, but others grow without it (anaerobic bacteria);
- **Food:** Protein, which could be proper food or just dirt;
- **Moisture:** Water;
- **pH (acid/alkali conditions):** Bacteria dislike extremes so they won't grow where it's too acidic (on pickles) or too alkaline (which is why soap works to clean them away).

How Do I Control the Growth of Bacteria?

Simply put, if you can control some or all of the six things above – time, warmth, oxygen, food, moisture and pH – then you will do well.

Do not leave hot food sitting around for too long (time) where it will start to cool and enter the danger zone (warmth). Put food in the fridge as soon as possible (controlling the warmth again). You might preserve some foods by removing oxygen (for example, by bottling it, or putting it in jars, or canning it). Don't feed the bugs (clean to remove dirt). Lack of moisture in some foods will prevent bacteria growing in them (jam, preserves); and don't leave damp cleaning cloths or mops about. Finally, some foods are preserved by controlling the pH, such as pickles.

What are Some Common Types of Bacteria?

You might have heard of salmonella, *E. coli*, *Clostridium perfringens* (one of the main causes of food poisoning), *Clostridium difficile* (a hospital-acquired infection), *Clostridium botulinum* (causes botulism, also used in Botox, by the way, as it acts by paralysing the muscle), *Campylobacter*, *Staphylococcus* or *Streptococcus*.

Most *E. coli* strains are harmless, but some can cause serious food poisoning. The harmless strains are part of the normal flora of the gut. The bad news is that if the harmless ones are found in food, then that shows that the food has been contaminated with faeces. Yuck!

Most *Staphylococci* are harmless. This bacteria is normally found on the skin and mucous membranes of humans and other animals. So if it's in your food, it possibly means that someone hasn't been washing their hands after blowing their nose. Eeeooow!

While many types of *Streptococcus* are harmless, you will be familiar with the one that causes 'Strep throat'. If *Streptococcus* is found in your food, it possibly means that someone may have coughed into your food or hasn't been washing their hands after coughing. Not nice!

What is Food Poisoning?

Food poisoning is an illness that occurs usually between six and 36 hours after eating poisonous or contaminated food. Symptoms include vomiting, nausea, diarrhoea, abdominal pain and even death in extreme cases.

Food poisoning can be caused by bacteria, viruses, chemicals, metals (such as lead or mercury) and poisonous plants, such as the foxglove (*digitalis*) or poisonous mushrooms or toadstools.

How Do I Reduce Bacteria in the Food I Make?

There are three ways to reduce bacteria in the food you make:

- **Food hygiene management:** To make sure the food does not get contaminated;
- **Personal hygiene management:** Keeping yourself clean;
- **Environmental hygiene management:** Keeping your workplace clean and tidy.

Each of these will be controlled by your HACCP system that we discussed earlier. When you do your food hygiene training course (which is required by law), then all will be explained in more detail.

Hygiene

Hygiene refers to the practices and procedures essential to the maintenance of health and the quality of life. Keeping things clean and uncontaminated, in other words.

Why Bother?

If you don't have good hygiene practices when you prepare food, whether for yourself or for sale, then you run the risk of causing food poisoning. That's not good for your customer and not good for your reputation or your business.

Personal Hygiene

Good personal hygiene includes keeping your body clean (shower regularly), washing your hands regularly, wearing clean clothes and not engaging in unhygienic practices such as smoking, coughing or sneezing over food or people, picking your nose, ears, cuts, etc., nail-biting, using your finger to taste food, or spitting.

The big thing to remember here is WASH YOUR HANDS! You must always wash your hands:

- **Before:**
  - Starting work;
  - Handling food;
  - You move on to the next task;
- **Before and after:**
  - Treating wounds or cuts;

- o   Touching a sick or injured person;
- o   Inserting or removing contact lenses;
- **After:**
  - o   Using the toilet;
  - o   Handling raw food, especially meat;
  - o   Touching your face, nose, ears, hair, mouth, cuts;
  - o   Smoking;
  - o   Handling waste;
  - o   Cleaning duties;
  - o   Meal breaks;
  - o   Sneezing, coughing, or blowing your nose;
  - o   Handling money.

A carrier is a person who harbours, and may pass on, harmful bacteria, even though that person may show no signs of illness. If this person has poor personal hygiene and they handle food, then they might easily pass on the harmful bacteria to someone else.

5

PRODUCT DEVELOPMENT

Introduction

Wherever you get your ideas or whatever your motivation, you need to think things through before ploughing ahead. This will allow you to develop a better sense of what the product will be and how it will be sold. The more time, thought and energy that you give to this process at the start, then the higher the chances of success.

Your resources (financial, human, facilities) are limited, especially at the beginning of a project. So it is important to spend resources wisely: by being careful and thrifty at the start of the project, you will ensure that there will be enough time, cash and effort to keep going.

Questions you should consider:

- **What are you going to make / produce?** This is your first priority. Be clear what you want to do and why you want to do it. It will work out best if you enjoy what you are doing, and are good at it. Ideally, when looking at the local market, see whether there is a gap that you can fill with your delicious food. For example, despite a competitive market, there are market opportunities for Irish ice cream-makers. Ice cream is often regarded as an 'affordable indulgence' and suits the trend towards home entertainment;

- **Who / what is your target market?** Is it families, individuals, older people, children, single people, married couples, men, women, healthy eaters, dieters, indulgers, students, workers or …?

- **Who are your competitors?** Everyone has a competitor. Even makers of sausages with high meat content have competition from poorer quality sausages – if the consumer is offered a choice, they

may go for the cheaper option after all. Know who your
competitors are, where they are, and how you might steal away
some of their customers. Carry out a benchmarking exercise: What
do your competitors do well that you might do too, and what are
their weaknesses? You can compete with them by shouting about
your strengths, the great traits/flavours/quality of your food.
Where do your competitors sell their goods? Will you be there too
or will you sell somewhere else?

- **How will you make the cheese / bread / jam / hummus?** Can you
  get the necessary ingredients and have you a recipe?
- **What equipment / premises are needed?** Will your existing
  kitchen equipment do or must you buy new equipment?
- **Where will the food be sold?** Provide a local service also to build
  recognition – collections from your house, deliver to local shops,
  supermarket, sell at farmers'/country markets and agricultural
  shows (see **Chapter 6**);
- **How much should you charge?** You need to compare the selling
  price of your food to similar products on the market. The
  consumer may expect to pay more for artisan food, but you need to
  prove it's worth the extra. Also, make sure you are not
  undercharging – don't forget to work out how much it costs you to
  make so that you don't make a loss;
- **On what occasions will the food be eaten?** Meal times, picnics, on
  the go, special occasions … this will affect the way you present and
  package the food, whether there is one, two or six items in a pack
  for example, as well as the type of packaging itself;
- **What are your packaging options?** Can you use plastic, paper,
  glass, jars, tubs or bags? Should you put one, two or six items in a
  pack, for example? Should you offer the option of single packs and
  multi-packs? If you already have your foods in shops, then think
  about pack sizes, formats and packaging for existing lines;
- **Is the product seasonal?** How do you manage in winter or off-
  season? Can you buy-in ingredients from elsewhere when you
  don't have them in your own garden, for example? Can you adapt

the product for different times of year? Can you introduce limited edition or seasonal varieties such as a turkey and ham pie at Christmas, lamb and mint for Easter, or bacon and cabbage for St. Patrick's Day?

- **How much of an income can you hope to get from making and selling these foods?** Is this going to be extra money for you or do you want to have a business that will provide you with a proper income? Either way, you must work out your costs (this is all covered in detail in **Chapter 8**).

Now Develop the Recipe and Method
Once you decide what it is you want to make, then spend some time developing your recipe and method. Do plenty of trials to make sure you can manage making just more than one or two at a time. Your kitchen equipment might be fine at the beginning, but might not last if you are using it long term or for larger sizes/quantities. Or your recipe may not scale – for example, if you increase the size of a cake from 6" to 9" or 12", and you use the same recipe, it might not turn out the same. You may have to alter your recipe and method for larger sizes – trial and error again.

New Product Development
You might have heard about new product development (NPD) models or perhaps the phrase 'stage gate'. These are just ways of managing the way in which new foods, or indeed any new products, are developed. The idea behind any development system is to make sure you avoid wasting your resources (time, energy, money) as far as you can.

Typical steps are:

- **Idea generation stage:** How to come up with new ideas (see above);
- **Feasibility stage:** Desk research, check out the market – is there anyone else local doing what you want to do? Look at your resources: do you have the time, money, knowledge, ability, kitchen, equipment etc. that you need?

- **Concept development:** Production of samples, do trials, test them out on your family and friends;
- **Business case:** A more detailed look at your target market, sales (how and where are you going to sell your food?), production (how and where are you going to make this food?), human resources (will it be just you or will you have help, and who is going to do what?) and financial issues (can you afford to start-up? can you get a grant?);
- **Further development:** Getting on with bigger batches, check any technical issues (you may need to tweak your recipe, like in the cake example above);
- **Launch:** Introduce your new product to the market – in effect, this probably means putting a few loaves, jars, buns, cakes or whatever into your car or the basket of your bicycle and bringing them up to the corner shop where your local friendly shopkeeper has agreed to take a few to try them out and see whether they sell;
- **Project performance review:** Look at everything every now and then and see whether you want to make any changes. Can you get cheaper/better ingredients? Can you make bigger batches? Can you add to the range? Can you save on costs anywhere without compromising your quality?

Processing Partners – Outsourcing Production

Here you look at a simple question: Will you make your food product yourself or get someone else to do it for you?

It is not unreasonable to consider outsourcing some of your production work. You might buy in readymade pastry cases, for example – unless you are very keen to make your own. If you can make really good pastry, then go ahead. But it is possible to buy very good quality frozen pastry, so don't rule it out. Some of the top chefs in the country buy-in their pastry.

If you are making sausages or meat products, you might develop the recipe and specify the ingredients, but perhaps you don't have a sausage machine. You could ask a butcher to make the sausages for you or ask him if you can have access to the machine when he is not using it.

The golden rule of any 'partnership' is trust and making sure that you can work with people for the long-term. The trust derived from relationships offers far more security than anything written down in a contract. All the same, you should ask your sub-contractor (the person/company who is going to make the food for you) to sign a non-disclosure agreement, which would give you some protection, but know that even a slight tweak to a recipe or a process might render this agreement null and void.

One step you should definitely take is to document your recipe and the detail of the required processes and send both to yourself by registered post and DO NOT OPEN the envelope unless you find yourself in a litigation process and only then open the package in a legal setting, solicitor's office or courtroom, with independent witnesses present. This is the most cost-effective method of proving ownership of the intellectual property (IP).

Sensory Analysis

Sensory analysis answers the critical question: How does it taste, look, smell and feel?

If you ever watch cookery programmes on television, you might notice that the good chefs taste their food as they go along. They want to make sure that there is a good balance of flavours, that it is seasoned correctly, that no one ingredient is overpowering – and they make adjustments accordingly. The same goes for the foods you are making for your new business. As you develop your recipe, taste it! Ask others to taste it too. Ideally, your tasters would be able to describe what they are tasting rather than simply saying they like it or don't like it without articulating why. Smokers do not make good tasters, by the way, as their taste buds are not sensitive enough.

Sensory analysis of food uses the five senses – sight, smell, taste, touch and hearing – either individually or in combination, to look at the characteristics of food:

• Appearance;

- Flavour;
- Aroma;
- Texture
- Sound.

Yes, sound! Dark chocolate snaps when you break it because it has a high percentage of cocoa solids. Or does anyone remember Space Rocks that popped and fizzed in your mouth? These are called the 'organoleptic' properties of food.

Appearance

We eat with our eyes first, so is your food visually appealing? Think about the colour, size, shape and shine. The colour of food is very important: does it look natural or artificial? Bright green vegetables look fresher, for example. The shape, size and appearance also influence consumers. When is mould acceptable? Fine in a blue cheese but not on bread! Wilted lettuce or carrots that have a wizened appearance are not acceptable either.

Flavour

Flavour has two parts:

- **Mouthfeel:** The coldness of ice cream or the burning sensation of chilli;
- **Taste:** Sensed by the taste buds on the tongue.

And there are four types of taste sensation:

- Sweet;
- Salt;
- Sour;
- Bitter.

By the way, sour and bitter tastes are often confused, so you need to be clear what your tasters mean when they describe the taste to you. Lemon juice has a sour taste whereas coffee has a bitter taste.

Aroma

Smell evaluates the aroma of food – the smell of freshly baked bread, for example – and is important in the appreciation of flavour. A pleasant aroma makes food appetising. To arouse a sensation of smell, a substance must be in a gaseous state. Smell is useful in detecting fresh, rancid or occasionally poisonous food.

Texture

Texture is a key quality for many foods – for example, think of the tenderness of meat, the softness of bread, the crunch when breaking into crème brulée or the chewiness of toffee. It includes the consistency, viscosity (thick or thin liquids), brittleness, chewiness and the size and shape of particles in food, like the texture of a pear that is gritty.

Sound

The sounds made by food during preparation and while eating it are important for consumers' decisions also, like the sizzle of fried food, the fizz of drinks, the crunch of raw vegetables, the cracking of hard biscuits or dark chocolate.

So, it is really very important to taste your food, to get others to taste it and to give you feedback and then to adjust your recipes as necessary.

Shelf Life

One of the best explanations I've heard recently to describe the difference between 'Best Before' and 'Use By' dates is that used by SafeFood: *Best Before is a guideline and Use By is a deadline.*

Shelf life is a guide for the consumer as to the length of time that food can be kept before it starts to deteriorate. However, the consumer must play ball and follow the stated storage conditions if the shelf life is to be achieved.

Is Shelf Life Related to Food Quality?

Yes, the food might be safe to eat after the expiry (Best Before) date, but it might be stale or mushy or flavourless. Since the Best Before date is related to quality (for example, taste, aroma, appearance), after that date the food may not be unsafe to eat, but it may not be pleasant to eat. Best Before is applied to foods that are low risk or are canned, frozen or dried, for example.

Is Shelf Life Related to Food Safety?

Yes, it is inextricably linked. Shelf life testing describes how long a food will retain its quality during storage. You use HACCP to control the growth of pathogens (bad bacteria). So the Use By date is all about the safety of a food product. It is relevant for perishable foods that may constitute a danger to human health after a short time. The accuracy of the Use By date is really important from a food safety point of view.

How to Work Out the Shelf Life of Your Food

The extent to which you have to do a 'shelf life study' depends on the food you are producing. Factors influencing shelf life of food include microbial growth (mould, bacteria, yeasts, etc.) and non-microbial spoilage caused due to the gain or loss of moisture from the food; any chemical changes that might occur; light-induced change (colour fading); temperature changes (which cause the whitening or 'bloom' in chocolate); physical damage that might occur over time if it gets crumbly or cracks form; or even other spoilage from rodents and insects, taint or tampering.

All these factors should be taken into account when working out your shelf life. If you are making low-risk foods like bread, jam, dips, etc., where public health is not a major issue, your own experience will inform you as to what the shelf life might be. For high-risk foods, though, you might have to send samples away to a microbiology lab for testing to measure how many bacteria are present that you need to worry about.

Can you carry out your own shelf life testing? Yes, you can do it easily for some types of foods, especially those where it's the eating quality that you are concerned about. Simply store the food in its packaging under the storage conditions it should be kept in, then take a sample every day or week or as often as you need to notice any changes. This will give you a guide as to when the food starts to deteriorate, and you can set the shelf life accordingly. If you're not sure, or if your food is perishable and where food safety is the issue, then get professional advice.

By law, you must state the Best Before or Use By date on your label. This is covered in detail in **Chapter 7**.

6

ROUTES TO MARKET, BRANDING AND A MARKETING PLAN

What Is A Route To Market?

The 'route to market' is a key element in relation to the development and launching of your own food – it's how you get your food on the consumers' tables! The first step in finding the best routes to market is to identify clearly what it is you intend to supply, and also to think about who you want to sell it to. You must know who your target customer is. Now you must ask yourself: Where are they located? How are you going to get your food into their shopping bag – and onto their tables?

You must compose and write down a short statement or business pitch that you will use to all your potential customers and retailers. It's good to prepare this in advance, since it will help you to be consistent rather than stumbling over your words every time you try to talk to someone about your new food venture. Include a clear description of the food's unique selling points (USPs).

The target market will influence which route to market you use. For most small-scale artisan producers, the target market is their local or regional area to begin with, selling to consumers who prefer local food and who are willing to pay a premium for it. These customers are likely to buy food from independent craft butchers, specialist shops, artisan stores and farmers' or country markets. In addition, customers within a radius of about 25km might buy *via* box schemes, farm-gate pick-ups and home deliveries.

Where Are Your Customers?

Before you even start thinking about your best route to market, ask yourself: Where do my potential customers shop? If you only sell in farmers' and country markets, are you missing out on a large number of shoppers who only shop in supermarkets? Where are people going anyway that you might be able to sell from? Consider regional airports, where travellers are always keen to take something back home either for themselves or as a gift; tourist attractions where there are large numbers of people herding through the gift shops; museums ... could you sell there? Well, you won't know unless you ask!

The development of garage forecourt shops in recent years has been extraordinary. Gone, for the most part, are the little draughty huts with a shivering petrol pump attendant. Instead, there are elaborate shops selling everything from windscreen wash to wine. If the travelling public is your market, eating-on-the-go, then remember to think about what packaging will best suit someone having lunch in their car.

The Supply Chain

It is important for food businesses to understand the supply chain with which they are involved. There are usually two types:

• Retailers (for consumer foods);
• Food service (for catering).

Alternative supply chains involve direct sales to consumers and many small producers start with this route – because they are short. Direct sales can include farmers' markets and online selling.

The diagram below shows two typical supply chains. There are three steps in the process between farm and consumer: each step in the process takes a slice of the 'money pie'. By using the direct sales route, some of the steps are eliminated, and with them, some of the costs.

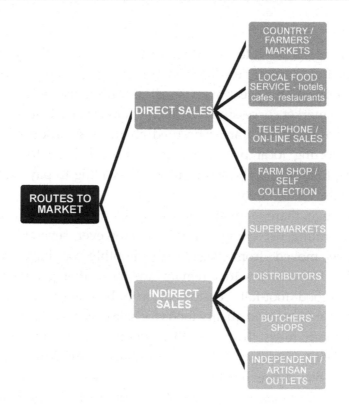

Route Options

The two main route to market options (and their sub-options) – for example, for a meat food producer – are:

- Direct sales:
  - o Country/farmers' markets;
  - o On-line sales – website, box schemes;
  - o Local food service direct to hotels and restaurants;
  - o Farm shop/collections by consumer;
- Indirect sales:
  - o Supermarkets;
  - o Butchers' shops;
  - o Food service distributors;
  - o Independent retailers/specialist shops/artisan outlets.

Direct Sales

Farmers' markets provide direct access to customers. This route is good for getting customer feedback and for carrying out initial tests of market/product and a great many small producers use or have used this route to market successfully. Farmers' markets attract local trade, bringing consumers who are concerned about mass-produced food, about supporting local producers, and who are keen to support minimising food miles. These consumers are willing to pay extra for these benefits. These are the 'foodies'.

At one stage, there were approximately 130 farmers' and country markets operating, according to Bord Bia. However, several of these either have moved from weekly to monthly or have ceased completely. The markets that remain are those that get plenty of customers (good foot-fall), customers who buy every week, and producers that have good quality foods for sale every week.

If you decide to try this route, then you need to be aware of the *Voluntary Code of Good Practice for Farmers' Markets 2009-2010*, available from Bord Bia (**www.bordbia.ie**). There is also lots of useful information in *The Village Market Handbook* from Irish Village Markets, which you can download free from the FSAI website (**www.fsai.ie**) or from **www.irishvillagemarkets.ie**. Bord Bia also publishes *A Guide to Selling Through Farmers' Markets, Farm Shops and Box Schemes in Ireland*, which again you can find on the Bord Bia website.

It is important to realise that, for most markets:

- Traders must carry their own public liability insurance;
- Traders might have to provide their own cover and equipment for displaying produce, as not all markets provide canopies and tables;
- Traders involved in the handling of food must comply with legislation, and some markets may ask you to show your HACCP approval certificate. Some EHO offices have published guidelines for food stalls, so ask in your local office.

Standing at a food stall is labour-intensive – it requires commitment in terms of stall staffing and management – and cash handing may be a risk factor.

From the perspective of the small food producer, direct selling *via* farmers' markets, box schemes and farm shops offers a number of advantages as a route to market. The supply chain is relatively short and there is direct contact with customers. This is a good way to start to build relationships with your customers, who will then recognise your food when they see it in their local shops. It also allows you to display your food the way you want it displayed, as you're not relying on shops to do a good job for you.

For the direct sales route, investment in equipment will be required. These requirements include table/canopy, mobile refrigerated unit and utensils. Transport requirements are generally far simpler than the more conventional routes to market and, in many cases, there are no intermediaries involved.

A growing number of producers and the increasing popularity of box schemes show that **telephone and online sales** are other potential routes. Good examples of online food sales in Ireland include Omega Beef Direct (**www.omegabeefdirect.ie**) and James Whelan Butchers (**www.jameswhelanbutcher.com**). Several other producers provide an ordering service by telephone.

Delivery of orders from online sales could be managed on a rotation basis by a group of producers in a local area. However, in practice, this does not often work out and most producers just deliver all their own produce themselves. Alternatively, the consumer might collect their order either from the producer, farm-gate/house/shop, or from a central distribution point.

This route to market is labour-intensive and requires good organisation and management, and a strong commitment from producers who are willing to travel and manage the ordering system. Website design and maintenance also need to be considered.

If you are able to make a quality product with your USPs clearly defined, then local restaurateurs who are motivated and interested in using and promoting local producers might be interested in a **local food service**. Some restaurateurs are prepared to pay a premium, especially those who are interested in provenance and promoting local food. Be careful though, make sure you arrange for cash on delivery if you can, or at least don't allow credit to build up.

Indirect Sales

Route to market options for indirect sales include:

- **Supermarkets:** SuperValu and Centra stores are supplied through the Musgrave Chilled Distribution System. However, individual shops in this supermarket group also purchase directly from local suppliers. Tesco also buys on a shop-by-shop basis, but producers must make their approach *via* head office, not to local outlets;

- **Butchers' shops:** Some butchers may be interested in discussing terms with local producers when a product is ready for supply, provided it does not compete with their own lines. In fact, it can be a good idea to explain to any shop owner or butcher that your products might bring in more customers, making it a win-win!

- **Independent retailers / artisan outlets / small distributors:** It is always worth talking to local independent retailers who may take small quantities initially to test the local market and to get feedback. You might have to agree to a sale or return arrangement (where you only get paid if the food sells, and you have to take back anything that doesn't sell) – this is quite common in fact. It's not a bad way to start since the shop owner is not taking on any risk and so may be more inclined to accommodate you;

- **Alternative routes:**
  - *Events:* There are many annual Christmas markets and fairs around the country, food festivals, Bloom in the Park, agricultural and County Shows and so on. These provide a chance for consumers to try out new products, and for producers to test the market without having to make a longer term commitment to a market, week in week out;
  - *Weddings:* If you plan to make products for the wedding market, then it's wedding fairs you should target, as well as shops selling wedding dresses, suit hire, florists or anything associated with the event – and don't forget hen parties!

 o *Celebrations:* If you plan to make celebration cakes for birthdays, first holy communions, christenings or other family occasions, then leave cards or flyers in children's play centres, clothes shops, babywear and baby equipment shops and so on.

Distribution

Product distribution is generally a major obstacle for start-up producers. Unless you intend to distribute products yourself, then you will have to find a distributor. Options include food wholesalers, chilled foods distributors – such as Pallas (**www.pallasfoods.eu**), Crossgar Foodservice (**online.crossgar.ie**) or Musgrave Food Services (**foodservices.musgrave.ie**) – and many others.

Other distributors also have expressed interest in new niche, high quality, artisan food products. Some examples include: Independent Irish Health Foods Ltd. (**www.iihealthfoods.com**); Brandshapers (**www.brandshapers.ie**); M&K Meats (**www.mkmeats.eu**); Wholefoods Wholesale (**www.wholefoods.ie**) and others.

Get out the phone book, keep an eye on the lorries delivering to your local shop and approach the driver, or check out Bord Bia's *Guide to Distribution for Food and Drink Producers in Ireland.*

Distribution comes at a cost, and so most producers cover the distribution themselves initially. This is hard work, so you should try to plan your week and your route to be as efficient as possible.

Branding

Earlier, we talked about provenance and the importance of letting your customers know where your food is made. The next step is to promote this through your branding. The Fuchsia brand of food, tourism and crafts in West Cork (**www.fuschiabrands.com**) is a good example of how regional branding has been used to promote a group of producers under one umbrella.

Branding is always aligned to quality. A strong brand provides familiarity and creates an expectation in the mind of your customer about the level of quality in the product. Familiar food brands in

Ireland have strong associations for people, such as the old Quinnsworth Yellow Pack (low quality) or Superquinn's own brand (high quality). The Love Irish Food brand (**www.loveirishfood.ie**) uses a group image of quality for various producers, large and small.

Branding vs Labelling

What is the difference between branding and labelling? There are important differences between them. Food labelling is used to inform consumers of the properties of pre-packaged food. The most important rule of labelling is that the consumer should not be misled. The brand, however, is the trade name, an identifiable mark, with associations of quality and performance. A label is functional and its main purpose is to provide specific information, although a good label can enhance a brand also.

Logo

Differentiation is very important so that your customer does not mix your foods up with someone else's, and buy their product by mistake. As you may have a number of similar competitors, it is essential that your brand has a marked difference. Graphic designers will advise that you should be brave and make a real statement, by having something different rather than creating a 'me too' brand. For example, take a look at Ben & Jerry's ice cream branding. This brand was developed in the 1970s, and still looks fresh and full of personality today. Brave branding offers a real opportunity to create a mark of difference between yourself and your competitors.

Trade marks

Trade marks are symbols (like logos and brand names) that distinguish goods and services in the marketplace. A trade mark must be distinctive for the goods and services you provide. In other words, it must be recognisable as a sign that differentiates your goods or service from someone else's. A trade mark is the means by which a business identifies its goods or services and distinguishes them from the goods and services supplied by other businesses.

A trade mark may consist of words (including personal names), designs, logos, letters, numerals or the shape of goods or of their packaging, or of other signs or indications that are capable of distinguishing the goods or services of one undertaking from those of others.

Examples of familiar Irish trade marks are: Kerrygold, Glanbia, Tayto, Siúcra (bearing in mind that no sugar is processed in Ireland anymore!).

Talk to the Patents Office (**www.patentsoffice.ie**) for more information.

Defining your brand

The provenance, unique selling points and product characteristics should be captured in your brand. Areas to consider when developing your brand include:

* Core brand values: Functional, emotional, coherence, consistency, credibility, innovation, co-operation, belief, partnership;
* Where you see the brand going.

It is important to remember that every element reflects the brand, whether it is your packaging, press releases, personality or communication.

If sub-branding (a 'Lite' version of your product, for example) is needed, ensure that it enhances the brand. Sub-brands often can weaken and confuse an overall brand.

Competitive Advantage

A strong brand can provide competitive advantage in the marketplace. Your competitors may be trading also on quality, local, and artisan issues. Competition from large suppliers to supermarkets has to be considered, too.

Distinctive Values – Brand Recognition

Brand recognition is the extent to which a brand is recognised for its stated brand attributes or communications. Consumers will make associations with certain brands, both good and bad. Your food will need to communicate its brand along with the provenance, USP and logo in order to earn recognition.

Unique Selling Points

Everyone can come up with several unique selling points (USPs) for their product, which should be exploited in order to increase the value of your food to the trade and the consumer.

In order for the customer or consumer to be convinced to buy your food, then the USP must be clear. A USP defines a product's competitive advantage and is essential to identify what makes your food different from your competitors. These advantages must be emphasised every time you talk about your food to anyone who will listen!

Provenance

For food businesses, it is really important that your provenance story is communicated well both on your packaging and through all other communication channels – website, Facebook page, blog or wherever. Focusing on provenance and local sourcing provides Irish food producers with an opportunity to differentiate themselves from competitors. An example of companies using provenance to their advantage is the Love Irish Food (**www.loveirishfood.ie**) campaign. Bord Bia promotes Ireland as the Food Island in international marketing campaigns – just look at the Bord Bia channel on YouTube.

Examples of food provenance will continue to be important, in particular for locally-produced food. This may be driven in part by the expectation that local food is fresher, but also the recession has made shoppers increasingly keen to support local producers if they can.

In 2007, Bord Bia found that seven out of 10 shoppers prefer to buy local food, with 93% of those that buy local doing so because they want to support the local economy. In addition, 29% source their local food from farmers' markets, 35% from local supermarkets and 23% from larger supermarkets. The overall findings indicated that consumer demand is for authenticity, with health, naturalness and freshness being the primary motivating factors for purchase. According to the research, three out of four Irish grocery shoppers claim to buy local food because "they want the most natural kind of food they can get".

So, the provenance relating to your food products needs to be clearly defined. Take a look at some tourism websites, which are great at describing lush heathery mountainsides, sea spray, wild landscape and all that good stuff!

A Marketing Plan

Marketing usually looks at the following:

- **Business profile:**
  - o Organisational structure;
  - o Products and services; and
  - o Strengths, weaknesses, opportunities and threats (SWOT);
- **Industry analysis:**
  - o Environmental factors: Political, economic, social, technological, legislative and environmental (PESTLE);
  - o Demographics;
- **Customer analysis:**
  - o Target market;
  - o Market size;
- **Competitor analysis;**
- **Marketing strategy;**
- **Marketing mix:** The four Ps (product, place, price and promotion), plus process, physical evidence and people where you are selling services.

All of these lead to your marketing plan, a critical document.

Marketing is the assessment, creation and meeting of demand. The more detailed the market research, the sounder, more reliable the rest of your business planning will be. We will not consider marketing any further here, since it's a huge topic in its own right. But recognise its importance and look out for training courses or marketing mentors in your area to help you if necessary.

Food Awards and Competitions

Entering your food product into any of the many food awards and competitions is a great way to get free promotion and PR for you and your food business. Relatively new in Ireland are the Blas na hÉireann Awards but many producers also enter – and win – in the UK Great Taste Awards. So you should definitely take a look at these:

- Blas na hÉireann Awards / National Irish Food Awards (**www.irishfoodawards.com**);
- Good Food Ireland (**www.goodfoodireland.ie**);
- Great Taste Awards (**www.finefoodworld.co.uk**).

There is also an annual award from the Irish Food Writers Guild, details of which can be found at **www.irishfoodwritersguild.ie**. Euro-Toques also has awards, with details of past winners available on **www.euro-toques.ie**.

If you get shortlisted, even if you don't win, it's great for your profile and it's all free advertising!

7

LABELLING, NUTRITION CLAIMS AND ALLERGENS

Food Labelling

Food labelling is used to inform consumers of the properties of **pre-packaged** food. In other words, if your food is in a packet, bag, carton, jar or bottle when it leaves your kitchen, then it must have a label on it. If food is sold loose, like in a bakery, or deli counter or market stall and you put it into a bag when you're handing it over to the customer, then it doesn't need a label.

The most important rule of labelling is that the consumer should not be misled. The label cannot make any claims about a food's ability to prevent, treat or cure a human illness – snake-oil salesmen take note!

'Labelling' means any words, trade marks, brand name, pictures or symbols relating to the food and placed anywhere relating to the food. The information on the label must be easy to understand, be clearly legible, it must also be indelible, easy-to-see and not obscured in any way. Food products, including food imports sold in Ireland, must be labelled in English (with optional labelling in Irish).

There is specific labelling legislation for:

- Beef;
- Fish;
- Products with meat as an ingredient;
- Jams, jellies and marmalades (see **Chapter 11**);
- Foods containing quinine or caffeine;

- Food supplements;
- Alcoholic beverages.

Some of these are covered below. For the others, ask your EHO or DAFM vet or look them up on **www.fsai.ie**.

For example, specific regulations apply for the labelling of pre-packaged meat products, so if you are planning to produce meat products then make sure you download the FSAI *Guidance Note 17* from **www.fsai.ie**.

There is an exception to the rule for small packages or containers where the largest surface is less than $10cm^2$ (such as chocolate wedding favours) – in this case, only the name of the food, the net quantity and date of minimum durability are required.

However, it is also recommended to provide information on allergens where applicable.

At the moment, there are no specific requirements about the minimum font size for the mandatory information listed above for allergen labelling or foods sold unpackaged, or labelling requirements regarding foods sold *via* the Internet. However, new legislation comes into effect in December 2014, which specifies a font size where the x-height is equal to or greater than 1.2mm (your graphic designer will know what this means). And, in the case of packaging or containers, the largest surface of which has an area of less than $80cm^2$, the x-height of the font size must be equal to or greater than 0.9mm.

The FSAI publishes *The Labelling of Food in Ireland 2007*, which has all the information you need to start with.

What Must Appear on the Label?

There is a mountain of legislation about food labelling. However, you should start with general labelling legislation, which says that the following must appear on the label:

- Name under which the product is sold;
- List of ingredients;
- Quantity of certain ingredients;
- Net quantity;

- Date of minimum durability;
- Special storage instructions or conditions of use;
- Name or business name and address of the manufacturer, packager or seller within the EU;
- Place of origin of the foodstuff if its absence might mislead the consumer;
- Instructions for use if necessary;
- Beverages with more than 1.2% alcohol by volume must declare their actual alcoholic strength.

There are many exceptions and special cases for all elements of the labelling legislation. What is described here is for food in general. It's a good idea to check your labels specifically with your EHO.

Name Under Which the Product is Sold

This means its customary name, say 'shepherd's pie' or the name that describes what it actually is, like 'vegetable soup'. If you call your product something vague like 'Mary's Winter Casserole', then you'd have to put a line underneath describing it so that customers know exactly what it is.

So, this element of your label might look like:

Mary's Winter Casserole
Beef and vegetables in gravy

List of Ingredients

The ingredients should be listed in descending order of quantity, starting with the ingredient with the largest amount in your recipe. In addition:

- Products requiring reconstitution may be listed as dehydrated or rehydrated;
- If you use additives, then you can either use the E number alone or the name, or both, as you prefer – for example, 'thickener (E412)', 'thickener (Guar Gum)' or 'thickener (E412/Guar Gum)';
- For compound ingredients (ingredients that have more than one component themselves, such as the pastry in a fruit pie or

mayonnaise in coleslaw), you must list their ingredients separately too unless they are less than 25% of the final product – and there are some other exceptions;

- The amount of added water need not be listed as an ingredient if it does not exceed 5% by weight of the finished product;
- If you are using water for ingredient reconstitution (in other words, using it to reconstitute dry ingredients before adding them into your sausage mixture, for example) or if the water is not going to be eaten (like tuna or olives in water), then you do not have to declare it as an ingredient;
- If your food contains certain allergens (ingredients that are known to cause an allergic reaction), then you must mention them specifically on the label, by law, so that the consumer knows they are present. Allergens are covered in more detail further on in this chapter.

Quantity of Certain Ingredients
This is called QUID, short for 'quantitative ingredient declaration'. What it means is that, in certain instances, the percentage of specific ingredients is declared on a label if the name of the food implies that the food contains a specific ingredient.

Some examples:
- Pineapple yogurt – declare the percentage of pineapple;
- Irish Stew – declare the percentage of lamb;
- Chilli con Carne – declare the percentage of beef;
- "with cheesy topping" – declare the percentage of cheese;
- Leek and Potato Soup – declare the % leek and % potato.

The image below is the back panel from a 'Cheese and Tomato Quiche'. As you can see, the full legal name of the food is 'Medium mature cheddar cheese, red cheddar cheese, mozzarella and tomato combined with a creamy egg custard encased in a crisp shortcrust pastry'. The ingredients list therefore must declare the various ingredients listed in this name. In this case, the percentage of **cheese,** egg, **tomato** and **cream** are given. In addition, the label also gives the percentage of **onion**.

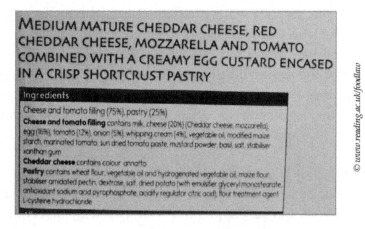

MEDIUM MATURE CHEDDAR CHEESE, RED CHEDDAR CHEESE, MOZZARELLA AND TOMATO COMBINED WITH A CREAMY EGG CUSTARD ENCASED IN A CRISP SHORTCRUST PASTRY

Ingredients

Cheese and tomato filling (75%), pastry (25%)
Cheese and tomato filling contains milk, cheese (20%) (Cheddar cheese, mozzarella), egg (16%), tomato (12%), onion (5%), whipping cream (4%), vegetable oil, modified maize starch, marinated tomato, sun dried tomato paste, mustard powder, basil, salt, stabiliser xanthan gum
Cheddar cheese contains colour annatto
Pastry contains wheat flour, vegetable oil and hydrogenated vegetable oil, maize flour, stabiliser amidated pectin, dextrose, salt, dried potato (with emulsifier glyceryl monostearate, antioxidant sodium acid pyrophosphate, acidity regulator citric acid), flour treatment agent L-cysteine hydrochloride

© www.reading.ac.uk/foodlaw

Another example is this packet of 'Yogurt Coated Nuts and Raisins'. Since the words 'yogurt coated', 'nuts' and 'raisins' appear in the name of the food, the ingredients list must declare the percentage of these used. It was considered unnecessary to declare the percentage of the various types of nuts.

QUID is not required if the percentage declaration is covered by other legislation, like in the case of jam

Yogurt Coated Nuts & Raisins

Yogurt coated peanuts, almonds, hazelnuts and raisins

e 200g

Ingredients

Yogurt coating (66%), nuts (26%) (peanuts, almonds, hazelnuts), raisins (8%)
Yogurt coating contains vegetable fat, sugar, yogurt powder, skimmed milk powder, whey powder, glazing agent gum arabic, emulsifier soya lecithin

© www.reading.ac.uk/foodlaw

(see below). However, you might like to declare all the vegetable percentages if you are producing a mixed vegetable soup, for example, because it implies freshness.

Net Quantity

The net quantity means the weight of the food without its packaging. Some products are exempt from weight marking, such as herb packs weighing less than 5g, or sugar confectionery of less than 50g.

In 1981, Ireland introduced the average system of weight control denoted by the **'e'** mark. What this means in effect is that the weight of the food is an average weight.

For example, let's say your pre-packed bag of buns has a stated weight on the label of 250g. Then if you weighed 10 bags of buns, on average, each bag would have to weigh 250g, even if some were a little bit more and some a little bit less. If you want to start getting into the complexities as to how much a 'little bit' actually means, you can check out the legislation in detail (*EC Packaged Goods (Quantity Control) Act, 1980* and *Packaged Goods (Quantity Control) Act, 1981*).

Date of Minimum Durability

The difference between Best Before and Use By dates was covered in the Shelf Life section of **Chapter 5**. As described by SafeFood, Best Before is a *guideline* and Use By is a *deadline*.

The rule of thumb is that Use By is for perishable foods that might cause food poisoning or illness because they are likely to contain unacceptable levels of bacteria or other microbes after a time.

Generally, foods that must be kept in the fridge to maintain their safety rather than their quality, and that have a relatively short shelf life after they have been made, require a Use By date – for example, ready-to-eat foods or foods that must be cooked or reheated before eating, such as meat, fish, poultry, as well as some dairy products.

Again, there are some exceptions, so check out what's right for your food.

Special Storage Instructions or Conditions of Use

If the food must be kept in the fridge or in a cool dry place in order to maintain its shelf life, then you need to put this message on the label to tell the consumer what they have to do when they get the food home.

You also should mention how long to keep the pack once opened, or whether they need to store it in the fridge once opened.

Other Items

Other information that should be included in your labelling includes:

- **Name or business name and address of the manufacturer, packager or seller within the EU:** You should use a postal address, as a website address is not acceptable on its own. *Very important to note – even if you outsource your production to someone else (a third party), it is YOUR name and address that should be on the label, not theirs;*
- **Place of origin of the foodstuff:** This should be clear if its absence might mislead the consumer to a material degree – you only need to do something about this if, for example, you make 'Italian sausage', but you make it in Cork, or you make Brie cheese (typically a French cheese) in Tipperary. It needs to be clear on the label where the food was made. As long as the consumer doesn't think it came from some place it didn't, then that's fine;
- **Instructions for use (where necessary):** This is where you tell the customer how to cook or reheat the food, whether it's suitable for frying or baking, whether it should be thawed before use, etc;
- **Actual alcoholic strength:** Beverages with more than 1.2% alcohol by volume must declare their actual alcoholic strength.

For example:

Monnie's Fine Foods
Farmhouse Vegetable Soup
Ingredients: Potato, Parsnip, Carrot, Onion, Garlic, Vegetable Stock.
Keep refrigerated. Made in a kitchen that uses nuts as an ingredient.
Use by: dd/mm/yyyy
Monnie's Fine Foods, Foodville, Co. Leitrim   e225g

Note that the following items must appear in the same field of vision on the label:

- Name;
- Net quantity;
- Date of minimum durability;
- Actual alcohol content (if over 1.2% alcohol by volume).

Nutritional Labelling

When you read a label and see a table that lists the protein, carbohydrate, fat and other nutrients in the product, this is nutritional labelling. At the moment, there is NO legal requirement to have this on the label. However, from December 2016, nutrition information will be mandatory for most pre-packaged foods – check with your EHO or the FSAI when the time comes.

However, many producers choose to label their foods with nutritional information to enable consumers to make more informed choices about the nutrition characteristics of the food, although most artisan producers don't do so, especially in the early days of their business. There are a couple of likely reasons for this:

- It might imply that the food is mass-produced (since the legislation requires that all ingredients must now be listed on pre-packaged foodstuffs);
- It costs money to analyse and list the various nutrients – and to print up the labels!

So how do you work out the nutritional analysis figures? There are three ways:

- Send the food off to a lab for analysis;
- Work it out by hand using your recipe and the tables of figures for the various ingredients from McCance & Widdowson's book, *The Composition of Foods*;
- Use special nutritional analysis software to work it out (NutriCalc and MicroDiet are common examples).

Any of these methods is acceptable. The first and third options will be done for you by someone who has a chemical analysis lab or who has the software (you're not expected to buy it yourself!). The second option is laborious, and it depends on how much you like getting stuck into calculations and formulae. It is entirely up to you to choose the method. But remember again, you don't actually have to go to this trouble at all unless you're making a nutritional claim for your food.

But if you claim that your food is high or low in fat or salt or calories or fibre, for example, then you have to be able to stand over it. The following are some examples of nutrition claims that are defined in the legislation:

- **Reduced fat:** 30% reduction compared with standard product;
- **Low fat:** Maximum of 3g/100g per product;
- **Reduced calories:** 30% reduction compared with standard product;
- **Low calories:** Maximum 167Kj (40 Kcal) per product.

For more about nutrition claims, look at the list in *Appendix VII* in the FSAI's *Labelling of Food in Ireland 2007* – it's all there.

If you decide to go down the road of declaring the nutritional information (as g/100g by the way), then the next step is to know whether your food falls into Group 1 or Group 2:

Group 1	Group 2
Energy (kJ / kcal) Protein (g) Carbohydrate (g) Fat (g)	Energy (kJ / kcal) Protein (g) Carbohydrate (g) *of which sugars (g)* Fat (g) *of which saturates (g)* Fibre (g) Sodium (g)
Group 1 format must declare the above where a nutrition claim is made for one or more of these nutrients.	Group 2 format must declare the above where a nutrition claim is made for one or more of these nutrients.

Health Claims

The other type of claim that is sometimes made is a 'health claim'. This is any claim that states, suggests or implies that a relationship exists between a food (or one of its constituents) and health (for example, "lowers cholesterol"). This is acceptable under law, provided there is scientific data to prove it (which can be difficult and expensive) or that the relationship has been around for so long that consumers understand it (for example, everyone knows that fibre is good for your digestion).

By the way, any health claim that states, suggests or implies that eating a particular food significantly reduces a risk factor in the development of human disease is prohibited!

For more information about health claims, and what you can or cannot say, refer to the FSAI website (**www.fsai.ie**) for its guidance document.

Allergens

The legislation also requires that the presence of recognised allergens must be clearly labelled, as shown here. If you want to read the legislation, it's in *Annex IIIa* of *Directive 2000/13/EC* and it lists the allergens as:

- Cereals containing gluten and products thereof;
- Crustaceans and products thereof;
- Eggs and products thereof;
- Fish and products thereof;
- Peanuts and products thereof;
- Soybeans and products thereof;
- Milk and products thereof (including lactose);
- Nuts – almond, hazelnut, walnut, cashew, pecan nut, brazil nut, pistachio nut, macadamia nut and Queensland nut and products thereof;
- Celery and products thereof;
- Mustard and products thereof;
- Sesame seeds and products thereof;
- Sulphur dioxide and sulphites at concentrations of more than 10mg/kg or 10 mg/litre expressed as SO_2;
- Lupin and products thereof;
- Molluscs and products thereof.

That's quite a list! So if you are unsure, ask for help from your EHO or FSAI or some other food science and technology expert.

Organic Labelling

There are particular requirements for the labelling of organic products. Information is available from one of DAFM's three approved certification bodies:

- Institute of Marketecology (**www.imo.ch**);
- Irish Organic Farmers and Growers Association (**www.iofga.org**);
- Organic Trust (**www.organic-trust.org**).

You also will get information about organic production from any of these and from DAFM.

Organic labelling includes requirements for displaying the organic certification license number, the symbol of the particular certification body with whom you are registered and more.

The use of claims of superiority of produce just because they are organic is not permitted. In the case of organic-processed produce, the criteria are as follows:

- Minimum of 95% by weight of total is certified organic material;
- Maximum of 5% by weight of total is from the permitted non-organically pronounced ingredient list.

Sometimes, you see labels declaring 'made using organic ingredients'. What this means usually is that, while the food producer themselves is not organic-certified, they buy organic-certified ingredients and use them in their foods.

Gluten-free

A product labelled 'gluten-free' must contain less than 20mg gluten/kg (< 20 parts per million (ppm)). This level is suitable for the most sensitive of coeliacs.

Foods that contain between 20 and 100mg gluten/kg can be labelled as 'reduced gluten, suitable for most coeliacs' or 'very low gluten'.

Contamination during the baking process is a major hazard in a kitchen that makes both gluten-free and gluten-containing foods. Control here is really critical and you really must get advice from your EHO and from the Coeliac Society (**www.coeliac.ie**) about your set-up. The Coeliac Society's Food List team works with producers to make sure they comply with the standards for 'gluten-free' and 'very low gluten' foods and that no cross-contamination occurs during the manufacturing process.

To ensure no cross-contamination, you will need:

- Dedicated equipment and utensils;
- Very high standards for cleaning;
- A very well-organised kitchen or bakery.

So how do you manage to control this? Why, through your HACCP system, of course (see **Chapter 3**)!

Organising your day is one way to manage making both gluten-free and other foods that contain gluten. You could make your 'gluten-free' products first or at the start of the production day when contamination from dust is at a minimum and all equipment and clothing are thoroughly clean. Then follow 'gluten-free'/'very low gluten' products with gluten-containing products before cleaning.

Otherwise, make the gluten-containing products on separate days from 'gluten-free'/'very low gluten' products with a thorough cleaning in between.

There is increased demand from consumers for gluten-free foods. While most people do not have coeliac disease and choose gluten-free for personal reasons, you must work to the highest standards so that if you say 'gluten-free' *on* the pack then it is gluten-free *in* the pack and that anyone with coeliac disease won't be at risk from your food.

Other Labels

Apart from the labelling requirements covered by legislation, what other labels might you put on your food?

Promotional labels like 'buy one, get one free', competition alerts to let the buyer know that they are in with a chance of winning something, awards labels shouting about your recent successes, flash labels to point out that your food is 'yeast-free' are some examples.

There is nothing from stopping you putting on any or all of these. Just be careful that it all doesn't get very crowded and unattractive-looking.

8

MAKING AND MANAGING MONEY

You don't need thousands of euros to start a small food business. The main thing in starting and maintaining a successful small food business is a drive and a passion for what you are doing. Everything else follows. However, you need to be sure that, having put in all the effort, you see some rewards.

Pricing and Margins

When you hear people talking about pricing models and margins, what do they mean?

Pricing is how much it actually costs you to make the product plus a margin for profit. Premium pricing is where your customer is willing to pay extra for something of special value to them. Consumers know that they usually get what they pay for, so cheap food implies poor quality and they expect to pay a bit more for artisan, good quality food. Margin is the slice (or slices) that everyone in the supply chain takes – for example:

- The producer (you) makes the product for €2;
- The distributor, who transfers the product from you to the retailer, adds on 50c;
- The retailer adds on €1.50;
- So the customer buys the product for €4.

It might seem to make sense to cut out the middle-men so that you, as the producer, can get the full retail price. When you are just starting out, you'll probably find that you have no choice here, as few distributors will take on an unproven product. However, as you get busy, then you will find it more time- and cost-effective to have someone to distribute and sell your foods – even though this means you receive less revenue for each sale.

The difficulty is in knowing what margin a shop or supermarket will want; often this comes down to hard-nosed negotiations. The bigger supermarkets have a set margin they apply and you might not have much say in that. Smaller shops may operate on a sale or return basis, so you only get paid if the product is sold.

Regardless of where you sell, look at what your competitors are selling their products for and then you can work around that price as a starting point for cost/margin calculations.

Costs

The costs that you must consider include some or all of the following:

- Ingredients, equipment (knives, scales, mincing equipment, cash till, etc) and packaging costs;
- Training costs, since at least one person will need to be trained in food hygiene;
- Food safety costs, including the cost of aprons, gloves, hairnets, refrigeration units, temperature probes, cloths, detergents, soaps, towels, waste containers and so on;
- Stall set-up costs, including the stall itself, tables, canopies, banners, signs, display material with recipes, etc;
- Other capital items, including vehicle conversion;
- Distribution costs, to cover getting your food from your premises to the retailer and/or consumer whether you do it yourself or pay someone else;
- On-line selling skills, in addition to website development, domain registration, someone (possibly even yourself) will need to be trained in website maintenance and e-commerce (selling over the web).

Recipe Cost Calculation

CHOCOLATE CAKE	A Weight (g)	B Cost / weight used €
Butter	175	0.84
Chocolate	100	1.11
Flour	200	0.25
Baking powder	5	0.02
Bicarbonate of soda	5	0.02
Ground almonds	100	1.05
Dark brown sugar	275	1.60
3 Eggs (1 egg = 60g)	180	0.85
Buttermilk	150	0.12
ICING		
Chocolate	90	1.00
Butter	40	0.19
Double cream	150	0.95
TOTAL INGREDIENTS	1470	**8.00**
Electricity		0.50
Labour*		6.50
Packaging		2.00
TOTAL COST TO MAKE		17.00
Add on distribution costs		1.00
Add on margin		6.00
Selling price (direct sales)		24.00
Add on retailer's margin		6.00
Selling price (indirect sales)		30.00

You must include payment for your labour. The majority of small food producers and indeed small businesses starting up forget this. But if you can't pay yourself, then you're not in business!

Now ask yourself: *Will a customer pay €30 for a chocolate cake?* The answer depends on why they are buying it. If it is a large cake for a special occasion, then the answer is probably "Yes".

As you get into the swing of your business, you may be able to source the same ingredients more cheaply. Or you may be able to substitute cheaper ingredients without compromising the quality.

Running Costs per day for a Food Stall

Note that some markets charge more than others for the pitch.

		€
Rent of Stall	per day	25
Labour	8 hours/day/1 person @ €10/hr	80
Insurance	Estimate €1000 Per Year (26 weeks)	38
Fuel	For travel to/from the market	5
TOTAL cost per day before you sell anything!		148

Training

When it comes to managing finances, it is a very good idea to get help or to do a Start your Own Business course or get some other training to help you keep on top of things. You must keep track of your costs, expenses and sales. If you find yourself working very hard, selling tons of product and yet are left with no money for shoes at the end of the year, then there is something wrong somewhere. Either you're undercharging, or your costs are too high, or both.

Sometimes, you can get free training through FÁS, Skillnets or LEADER, depending on your circumstances.

Sources of Funding

The County and City Enterprise Boards (CEBs) (**www.enterpriseboards.ie**) and the Rural Development Partnerships (LEADER companies) (**www.nrn.ie**) may have funding to help you with feasibility studies, training or equipment. In addition, they have a list of experienced mentors with specialisms in food, finances, business start-up and more that you can access, often for free, but certainly for a small percentage of the actual cost. The CEBs also may provide funding for attendance at trade shows.

Enterprise Ireland has a great Innovation Vouchers scheme (**www.innovationvouchers.ie**), which is open to food businesses that are registered companies (sole traders are not eligible). The New Frontiers programme (**www.enterprise-ireland.com**) is Ireland's national entrepreneur development programme, funded by Enterprise Ireland and delivered at a local level by the Institutes of Technology.

Inter*Trade*Ireland runs an annual SeedCorn competition for start-up and early stage businesses as well as other funding for sales and marketing (Acumen programme) and for innovation (Fusion programme), once you're established and trading for a couple of years (**www.intertradeireland.com**).

The Food Works programme is a joint programme run by Bord Bia, Teagasc and Enterprise Ireland for new food start-ups (**www.foodworksireland.ie**). And check **www.bordbiavantage.ie** for more information on starting and marketing your food-based business.

My advice on funding – ask everyone! They will tell you quickly what is available and whether you're eligible or not. There are always new schemes, funding and training and mentoring programmes coming up. Don't assume anything – ask!

9

TRAINING REQUIREMENTS

As a food producer, you are required by law to have completed food hygiene training. A good starting point if you want to find a trainer is the Environmental Health Officers' Association (**www.ehoa.ie**), which lists all the registered trainers. FSAI has published booklets that outline the requirements for you and your staff in relation to training, so download them from the FSAI website (**www.fsai.ie**). Alternatively, ask your EHO about training.

Some sector-specific training courses and providers are mentioned in **Chapters 12** to **15**; other, more general courses and providers are listed below. Contact details are provided in **Chapter 16**.

If you are working on your own, then you will need to have a really good understanding of HACCP also. There are courses available for this too, usually one or two days in duration.

Note that, while the food hygiene course must be accredited, the HACCP course does not.

Food Hygiene and Food Safety (HACCP)

Food safety training is essential in ensuring the preparation and service of safe food. It is a legal requirement that anyone involved in making foods and working on food market stalls is adequately trained. You and your helpers (whether paid or unpaid) must have a knowledge and understanding of food hygiene and be able to demonstrate good hygiene practices. In addition, whoever is specifically involved in the design and implementation of the HACCP system must understand the principles of HACCP.

Regulation EC 852/2004, which covers the hygiene of foodstuffs, requires that food business operators (FBOs – that's you) must ensure:

- That food handlers are supervised and instructed and/or trained in food hygiene;
- That those responsible for the development and maintenance of HACCP have received adequate training in the application of the HACCP principles; and
- Everyone is trained in anything they're supposed to be trained in – ask your EHO to find out what applies to your products or check out the Training page on **www.fsai.ie**.

Sticking strictly to good hygiene principles is really critical when you are making your food products. You are legally obliged to ensure your food is safe for consumption. Food safety training is essential in ensuring the preparation and service of safe food.

Some providers of food hygiene and safety training are listed in **Chapter 16** and include:

- About Hygiene Ltd (**www.about-hygiene.com**);
- Alpha Omega Consultants Ltd (**www.alphaomega.ie**);
- Food Flow Training (**www.foodflow.ie**);
- Kennedy Food Technology ((086) 170 6939).
- The Food Technology Centre, St. Angela's College, Sligo (**www.thefoodtechnologycentre.ie**);

Most EHOA-approved trainers also deliver HACCP training.

After that, you can choose whatever training you like. Courses on everything from skills development (how to make cheese, etc) to personal development to sales and marketing training are available around the country.

Other Training

General training providers include:

- CAFRE (**www.cafre.ac.uk**);
- National Organic Training Skillnet (NOTS) (open to non-organic producers also) (**www.nots.ie**);

- Taste 4 Success Skillnet (**www.taste4success.ie**);
- Teagasc (**www.teagasc.ie**);
- The Food Technology Centre, St. Angela's College, Sligo: Food labelling and legislation, sensory analysis techniques, product development and more) (**www.thefoodtechnologycentre.ie**);
- The Organic Centre (**www.theorganiccentre.ie**).

Other Useful Courses

In addition, you might consider taking courses in:
- Packaging techniques;
- Product labelling and legislation;
- Sales and marketing;
- Financial management for the small producer / business;
- Social media skills training (Facebook for business, Twitter, etc);
- IT skills development;
- Personal development/confidence-building;
- Product development, creativity and innovation;
- Sector skills – baking, sausage- and cheese-making, jam making, yogurt and ice cream courses;

and there are many more.

10

BREAD AND BAKING

Opportunity

Most people I talk to who are considering starting up a food business at home are thinking about baking bread – usually brown bread. If not bread, then cakes, or buns. There are not as many apple-tart bakers! By the way, 'pie' (as in 'apple pie') is more American and usually denotes a product having a top crust.

While bread is an easy food to produce at home, you must ask yourself this first: Is there really an opening for yet another bread baker? What could I bake that's a little different? Perhaps you should consider using spelt flour or rice flour, adding seeds or going after the health food or 'free from ...' market.

A great selling point can be to tell your prospective customers what your food does not contain! You might think people would know that traditional brown bread or soda bread is not made with yeast. But, why make assumptions? It's always good to point these things out to shoppers; it will catch their eye that way (a flashy sticker can be good here) and help you make sales.

So try to do something a little different from the usual. One supermarket owner told me recently that if one more person comes in his door with queen cakes, he'll run them out the door! The cupcake craze has probably reached its peak too. Check out what's available, and try to fill a gap.

Most bread, cakes and fruit pies will sell all year round. Some will sell only at weekends. There will be increased demand around traditional family events – first holy communion parties are big business in Ireland, especially now when the trend is to entertain the family at home rather than in a hotel or restaurant. You could put up a notice in your local shop and offer a dessert service.

There are broadly two different categories of breads, depending on the raising agent you use: Soda bread (traditional Irish) and yeast bread. Some people may have heard about the Chorleywood bread process, which is a high-volume process of making dough. The method was developed in 1961 by the British Baking Industries Research Association based at Chorleywood in England, and is now used to make the majority of mass-produced white sliced pans. Compared to the older bulk fermentation process, the CBP, as it is called, is able to produce bread in a shorter time. The quality suffers, though, in many people's opinion. Home-producers of white yeast bread will be competing with the mass-producers. You can't complete on volume or price, but you can complete on quality and craft.

Ingredients and Production Requirements

The ingredients are simple: Flour, salt, sugar (maybe treacle instead of sugar), seeds perhaps, yeast possibly ... there is no absolute list of ingredients for bread. And you can add almost anything to it to make it different. Push sprigs of rosemary into focaccia bread before baking, or chop up fresh rosemary and add it with freshly ground black pepper to plain white soda bread, or add cheese and onions or sundried tomatoes to scone mix. Get as fancy as you like or keep it simple. The possibilities are endless.

What You Need

You need:

- Suitable premises, approved by the HSE/EHO;
- A bowl – plastic, ceramic, whatever you like;
- A surface for rolling-out and cutting;
- An oven;
- A place you can leave the bread to cool;
- A room to store the baked result.

You could decide to buy a bread-maker – a machine that takes a lot of the chore out of the process. To see which machine to buy, look at **www.bestbreadmachinereviews.com**. Or you might prefer to stick with the truly hand-made method, elbow grease and all.

For packaging, you'll need tins, cake boxes, paper bags, plastic bags, foil trays, foil/paper inserts and trays for transporting the finished breads.

Set-up Costs
Set-up costs include the price of the equipment, although your own oven, bowls and tins may suffice to begin with.

Running Costs
The main running costs involved are ingredients, electricity and labour. Unless you plan to wrap the bread, you won't need any packaging or labels. As with everything else we have talked about, don't forget to include your own time into any cost calculations. The cost of marketing and distribution is extra.

Return on Investment
The price you can sell your bread/buns/scones/cakes for should be higher than commercially-produced varieties – consumers expect to pay more for hand-made, home-produced baked goods, provided the quality and taste are there. Check local shops and see what other similar goods are being sold for. Maybe you'll only sell cupcakes or desserts at weekends. Most shops will have a sale or return policy for baked goods ('returns'), so you will have to take home what doesn't sell at your own cost. Go easy initially with the volumes! Keep an eye out for which varieties sell and which don't – and don't forget that there will be seasonal demand too.

Current Trends and Future Developments
Spelt flour, rice flour, gluten-free, sour dough, rye ... never has there been such a variety of baked goods on the market. Some will come and go. Some will peak, be trendy for a while and then fall back to a

reasonable everyday level (you know who you are, cupcakes!). While some foods will always be a regular part of the grocery basket, some are seen as treats and luxuries and so these will be purchased less often. Your food will compete for sales against all varieties of baked goods, so keep an eye out for what the consumers are looking for. The health food market is a big one.

Gluten-free produce is experiencing a huge increase in demand. Are there suddenly more people out there suffering from coeliac disease? I don't think so! But many people find that they can't tolerate wheat very well, others simply don't eat wheat through choice. In the past, good quality gluten-free bread was hard to come by. However, improvements in baking techniques and availability of gluten-free and other flours has meant that good quality gluten-free breads are more readily available. By the way, spelt flour is not gluten-free!

In order for products to be 'gluten-free' (or very low in gluten) when they reach the consumer, you have to be absolutely sure that your baking process is tightly managed to prevent any contamination with gluten. Cross-contamination is the process by which a 'gluten-free' product loses that status because it comes into contact with something that is not 'gluten-free'.

The best way to manage this is to make 'gluten-free' products at the start of the production day when contamination from dust is at a minimum and all equipment and clothing are thoroughly clean. Alternatively, you could make your gluten-containing products on separate days from your 'gluten-free'/'very low gluten' products.

FSAI has a very detailed guidance note on its website (**www.fsai.ie**) about producing foods that are gluten-free.

Specific Labelling Issues

Gluten-free: A product labelled 'gluten-free' must contain less than 20mg gluten/kg (< 20 parts per million(ppm)). This level is suitable for the most sensitive of coeliacs. So if you bake bread and you want to label it as gluten-free, then you must be absolutely sure that it meets this limit. It's not just a matter of complying with the legislation, but it could have a detrimental health implication for a person with coeliac disease if you don't. If your product contains between 20 and 100mg gluten/kg, then you can label it 'reduced gluten – suitable for most coeliacs' or 'very low gluten'. These are legal terms by the way, not to be bandied about lightly!

'Wheat-free' does not mean that the product is gluten-free. The product may contain other gluten-containing cereals such as spelt.

Sometimes you may see on a package 'Made in a factory handling gluten' or 'May contain gluten'. This is not a legal requirement and not a recommended practice.

Case Studies

Cherry Blossom Bakery

In December 2010, Simon and Siobhan Stenson started Cherry Blossom Bakery (**www.cherryblossombakery.ie**) when they identified a gap in the market for good quality artisan breads and confectionery made with natural ingredients, without additives or preservatives. They also have created a range of products specifically for people who are coeliac or who have wheat intolerance.

After Simon lost his job in construction, he turned to what he loved, and decided to go to the renowned Ballymaloe Cookery School to update his culinary skills. He used his knowledge to create tasty additive- and preservative-free artisan breads and cakes for the supermarket shelves. Siobhan's background is in finance, so she looks after finance, sales and marketing and gets to let her creative side out by designing the brand and packaging.

In the beginning, they started off in the disused kitchen of a pub that had closed down (take note anyone wondering where you can access kitchen facilities!). The business soon outgrew the pub kitchen and Cherry Blossom Bakery moved into bigger premises in 2012.

Initially, Simon approached SuperValu in Westport and was soon in several shops across the West of Ireland. You now can find Cherry Blossom Bakery on shelves in Tesco, Dunnes Stores, SuperValu and many other shops.

The Foods of Athenry

Behind Paul and Siobhan Lawless'
multi-award-winning business, The
Foods of Athenry, is an enthusiastic
farm family, who like many farm

families baked breads, tarts and cakes for their own kitchen table
(**www.foodsofathenry.ie**). Siobhan started by asking a local
restaurant whether they would take her brown bread. The restaurant
took 10 loaves. The following week, the order was for 40 – and a food
business was born. The Lawlesses sold their dairy herd in 2004 and
the bakery moved into the now-empty milking parlour.

The business has evolved over the years and now they have two
separate bakeries: one baking with wheat and spelt and one baking
certified gluten-free. The Foods of Athenry now makes a wide range
of bakery products catering to many dietary needs, including gluten-
free.

The road was not smooth: a fire gutted all the hard work in June
2011. A case of 'man makes plans, God laughs'. But Paul and Siobhan
picked themselves up and got to it again.

The hard work and attention to detail has paid off. Since 2007, The
Foods of Athenry has been featured in the *Bridgestone Irish Food Guide*,
which lists the 'Best in Ireland' of artisan-produced foods. It is a
member of Good Food Ireland. And, between 2008 and 2012, it
carried off 25 taste awards for a cross-section of products, rubbishing
the myth that healthier food is boring or less tasty. The newly-
launched gluten-free range is in fun funky packaging, all the colour
on the outside!

Cannaboe Confectionery

Sharon Sweeney started making and
decorating cakes in her kitchen in
Ballinamore, Co. Leitrim, before
converting the adjacent garage into a
state-of-the-art bakery. She produces

high-quality celebration cakes, made to order, from the freshest ingredients. Cannaboe (**www.cacamilis.ie**) specialises in and is well-known for wedding cakes but also makes novelty cakes. At one stage, Sharon also produced handmade chocolates. More recently, she has produced two DVDs, which give a step-by-step guide on how to cover and decorate cakes from the comfort of your own home, along with tips and recipes. In addition, she posts on YouTube!

One thing that Sharon has always been strong on is updating her skills and over the years she has taken part in many cake, chocolate and skills development courses in Ireland and the UK.

Useful Resources

- Andrews Food Ingredients (**www.andrewsingredients.co.uk**);
- Bakery Bits (**www.bakerybits.co.uk**);
- Easy Equipment: For wicker bread baskets (**www.easyequipment.ie**);
- G&S Services Bakery Equipment Ltd (**www.gandsbakeryequipment.co.uk**);
- McGrath Bakery Services Ltd: New and used equipment (**www.mbs-ltd.org**);
- Scobie Bakery: For when you go big time! (**www.scobiebakery.com**);
- Sugarcraft.ie: A large selection of home-baking and cake-decorating equipment (**www.sugarcraft.ie**);
- The Knead for Bread (**www.thekneadforbread.com**).

11

JAMS, CHUTNEYS AND PRESERVES

Introduction

Two of the most popular foods to be made at home for sale locally are bread and jam. In recent years, many home-producers have started making brown bread, buns and cakes (see **Chapter 10**), as well as jam, chutneys, dips and other preserves. These types of food products are relatively low risk from a hygiene point of view, and fairly easy to make in your kitchen. People love home-made bread and jam and your local shop is a good outlet, especially since many of these products have a long shelf life. So, if you have fruit trees, bushes, or canes, a glut of rhubarb, or access to fresh fruit (whether from a local grower or a fruit distributor), then jam could be the start you are looking for.

One word of caution though: because it is relatively easy to make these products in your kitchen and because they are relatively low risk, then the danger is that everyone else will be doing it too, which will mean competition for you. So do something different – even just slightly different.

Opportunity

There are very many jam producers in the country: some large scale, some small. Don't let this put you off. If you have a good product and have no local competition from other home-based producers, then consumers will be happy to try your jam. What will make them buy it again? The usual suspects: quality, taste and flavour. So spend time developing your recipe.

If you can come up with a good recipe for strawberry jam, which is notoriously difficult to make as it doesn't set easily (since it contains low levels of pectin), then you could be on to a winner! Jams made with no added sugar (using fruit juice instead usually) are also very popular. The higher the fruit content in your jam, generally the better it will be.

Ingredients and Production Requirements

The basic ingredients required for making jam, jelly or marmalade are fruit, sugar, acid, pectin and water. As with all food products, the fresher the ingredients, the better the product. Use only the best quality fruit, ensure it is just ripe and not bruised or torn.

The acid and pectin content of fruit is important to consider as these are required in order to achieve a good 'set' in the jam when the mixture cools down. All fruits contain pectin, but some have higher quantities than others. Crab apples, gooseberries, blackcurrants and redcurrants are all rich in pectin, whereas strawberries, cherries and pears contain very low levels of pectin. Blackberries, plums and raspberries contain medium amounts of pectin. For fruits with low/medium amounts of pectin, you may need to add commercial pectin to the recipe in order to ensure a good set. This is added when the fruit has been cooked and the flesh and skin have softened.

To test for pectin content, take one teaspoon of the juice from the cooked fruit, place it into a clear glass and allow it to cool for a couple of minutes. Then add three teaspoons of methylated spirits. If a large firm clot forms, this indicates that the pectin levels are high and there is no need to add extra pectin. If you get a number of broken clumps, this indicates that there is insufficient pectin to get a good set, so commercial pectin should be added.

Follow the suppliers' instructions when using a commercial pectin, as often the boiling time will be shorter after sugar has been added. The acidity of the fruit pulp also will influence the set, and as with pectin, fruits also differ in their acidity. Citrus fruits are acidic, while many other fruits such as blackberries, plums and raspberries have medium amounts, and strawberries and cherries are not at all acidic.

When making jams with medium/low acid fruit, add one or two tablespoons of fresh lemon juice per kg of fruit at the beginning of cooking.

Commercial jams often contain less than 50g fruit per 100g. Home-based jam makers should be aiming for 60g fruit/100g jam or higher, ideally. The legal minimum requirement is 35g/100g generally, although blackcurrants and quinces can be 25g/100g and there are some other exceptions. The FSAI has a great guide called *Labelling of Jams, Jellies and Marmalade* on its website (**www.fsai.ie**).

'Extra jam' contains higher levels of fruit than the usual version. The additional fruit can be added in purée form.

Sometimes you will see labels on jam listing 'jam sugar' as an ingredient. This is sugar with pectin mixed into it. Jam sugar often contains citric acid also, which acts as a preservative.

The FSAI guide lists the permitted ingredients in jam. Some of these are very specific, depending on the type of jam you are making. For example, red fruit juices can be used only in jam manufactured from rosehips, strawberries, raspberries, gooseberries, redcurrants, plums and rhubarb. Check the guide if you're not sure.

Teagasc has produced a fact sheet *Small Scale Production of Fruit Preserves*, which you can find on its website (**www.teagasc.ie**, search for "Jam").

What You Need
You need:

- Suitable premises, approved by the HSE/EHO;
- A clean pot or vessel for boiling and simmering the fruit – don't use copper or unsealed cast iron pans as the natural acids in fruit will damage the surfaces of these pans, spoiling your jam/preserve;
- A method for sterilising the clean jars;
- An area where you can pour the hot jam into jars;
- A labelling area where the labels are applied to the jars after the lids are on;
- A room to store the packaged product.

Set-up Costs

Set-up costs include the price of the equipment, although your own pots and pans may suffice to begin with.

You will need space – although you might be surprised at first at how few jars you seem to get from a large amount of fruit and sugar and all your hard work!

Running Costs

The main running costs involved are ingredients (fruit, sugar, pectin, fruit juice if you are using it), packaging, electricity and labour. It is important that you include your own time into any cost calculations. Labour input can be high! The cost of marketing and distribution is extra.

You also will have to buy jars, lids, and labels. You must buy new jam jars every time. You cannot use recycled jars from your cupboard (or anyone else's cupboard!) for your jam enterprise.

Sterilising Jars

There are a number of different ways that you can sterilise jars: oven, microwave or dishwasher. Ask your EHO which one they would prefer you to use. The key thing to check, however, is that the jar must be absolutely clean first.

Return on Investment

The price you can sell your jam for will be higher than commercially-produced jam – consumers expect it to be more expensive. Check local shops and see what other home-made jam is being sold for. Around €2.99 or higher is not uncommon.

How to Make Jam and Preserves

Every jam-maker claims that they have a special skill when it comes to their own recipes, and perhaps they do! It's best to make jam in relatively small quantities to give you better colour, flavour and clarity. The overall method is more or less as follows:

Wash fruit well

↓

Place in a large pot with a little water and some lemon
juice (lemon juice is needed to release the natural pectin
for some fruits)

↓

Bring to a boil

↓

Add sugar (if you add it too soon to soft fruit with skins
such as blueberries, the skin becomes tough and the
fruit won't burst)

↓

Stir really well until all the sugar has fully dissolved

↓

Keep boiling until jam reaches 104-106°C, setting
temperature (use a jam thermometer)

↓

Remove from the heat and take off any scum (especially
for marmalade)

↓

Pour into clean sterilised jars straight away

↓

Put on lids immediately

↓

Allow to cool before labelling

To test jam to see whether it is cooked enough and will set, you can:

- Dip a wooden spoon into the jam, holding the bowl of the spoon
  facing you. If the jam is ready, then two or three large drops will

roll along the edge of the spoon forming almost a triangle of thick jam;

- Drop a teaspoon of jam onto a chilled saucer (chill the saucer in the freezer or fridge first); the jam should cool quickly to room temperature and thicken up;
- Put a spoonful of jam onto a plate, push the jam with your finger and if the skin wrinkles, then the jam is ready.

Otherwise, boil it up again.

Current Trends and Future Developments

Quince jam, port-flavoured cranberry sauce, mixed fruit jams, jellies and various savoury dips and chutneys are increasingly popular. Consumers expect a choice now, so if you want to differentiate yourself from the herd, then produce high-quality, good-flavour, seasonal varieties.

Local honey is also popular among shoppers, though the recent poor summers have reduced the volume of honey available.

Finally, who could have predicted that we would have hummus or pesto in our fridges as part of our weekly grocery shopping? These once exotic foods are now mainstream, and not just for parties and holidays. So if you like to make savoury rather than sweet stuff in jars, consider chutneys, dips and other preserves.

Specific Labelling Issues

Jam, Extra Jam, Jelly, Extra Jelly and Marmalade
The usual labelling information is mandatory as already described in **Chapter 7**. In particular, note the following:

- **The name under which the product is sold:** For example, 'Raspberry Jam';
- **Instructions for use where necessary:** Reduced sugar jams must be kept in the fridge.

The following labelling information is also mandatory under the specific labelling rules:

- **An indication of the fruit used in descending order:** For example, for rhubarb and ginger jam;
- **The fruit content:** By including the words 'prepared with Xg of fruit per 100g';
- **The total sugar content:** By the words 'total sugar content Xg per 100g'.

Where the residual content of sulphur dioxide exceeds 10mg/ kg, you must indicate its presence on the list of ingredients – though most home-producers won't need to worry about this at all.

Very important! The name of the product, the fruit content and the total sugar content must appear in the same visual fields and in clearly visible characters.

Honey

Many people now keep their own bees and once again, Teagasc has a useful factsheet on *Honey Production* on its website (**www.teagasc.ie**).

If you keep bees and produce honey for sale, then you must register with DAFM as a 'primary producer'. You can get the form from your local office or download it from **www.agriculture.gov.ie** (search for "Registration as a Primary Producer of Honey").

There are very specific rules relating to the labelling of honey. Products can only be marketed as 'honey' if they comply with the definition and compositional requirements as set out in the Directive (*Directive 2001/110/EC* relating to honey), and you can get more information about this from the FSAI (**www.fsai.ie**).

Some of the most common types of honey are as follows:

- **According to origin:** Such as blossom honey or nectar honey (honey obtained from the nectar of plants);
- **According to mode of production and/or presentation:** Such as chunk honey or cut comb in honey (honey that contains one or more pieces of comb honey).

The country or countries of origin where the honey has been harvested must be indicated on the label. If the honey originates in more than one EU Member State or third country, then the indication may be replaced by one of the following as appropriate:

- 'blend of EC honeys';
- 'blend of non-EC honeys'; or
- 'blend of EC and non-EC honeys'.

Case Studies

Sean Casey, Westport Grove Jams & Chutneys

After a lifetime working in the pharmaceutical and health care industry as a microbiologist and production manager, Sean Casey started making jam at home in his kitchen in 2008. He saw a gap in the local market and decided to focus on jams, as they are a low risk product. When I first met Sean  a couple of years ago, he told me that if there was nothing much on the television, he would wander out to the kitchen and cook up a batch. If anyone was looking for him, his family would know where he could be found!

What did he do? In his own words, he:

- Approached local shops to see whether there was an interest;
- Asked shops what cost they expected the product to be delivered to them for; he already knew their selling price;
- Looked for suppliers and determined his costs. He did a costed bill of material for each product as he needed to know what his margin would be;
- Contacted the HSE to get approval; they were very helpful and gave practical advice;
- Developed his own lot number and batch tracking system and supplied the HSE with this information;
- Went back to the shops to discuss labels and what they advised; he knew appearance matters as the product needs to attract attention;
- Used local suppliers where he could;

- Started from his domestic kitchen but was advised by the HSE that if the business took off, they would demand a dedicated facility;
- Sent samples to an approved micro lab to validate his expiration dates;
- Started barcoding his product as some of the larger customers requested it;
- Printed his own labels as it gave him greater flexibility;
- In December 2011, moved into a dedicated facility on his property (built behind the house);
- Started making sugar-free jams and some chutney in August 2012. He knew there was a demand, but it took him 12 months to figure out how to make them.

His future plans include:
- Upgrading his labels to facilitate getting into the luxury end of the market;
- Bringing out a new range to facilitate the luxury range and selling online;
- With the help of his wife, he is making nougat and will soon move into fruit pastes and develop a website to sell these online also

Note that no external finance was provided for this project. Sean used his own resources, started small and built up the business over the years.

Redmond Cabot, Red's Sauces

Redmond Cabot has had a varied career – from self-employed photographer, retail shop owner, restaurateur, through being  unemployed, surviving the recession crash, becoming a father and now having launched a new business and starting all over again. His energy and enthusiasm for his work cannot but have an effect on the people he meets. When Red describes the dips, pickles, hummus and chutney he makes, your mouth will water – I guarantee it. He'll talk about how he roasts the chilli peppers himself because it brings out the heat better, and how you will notice the flavour of the sage coming through at the end as you enjoy the beetroot and sage dip. A great salesman talking honestly about his high-quality, hand-made food.

Red started up in his kitchen at home, but it quickly took over everything and his EHO advised that he'd have to move into a bigger space or reduce his volumes. So he started building a unit behind his house. This took some time, as he did it himself with help from friends while at the same time making product and selling it in the markets. He eventually got it finished, which allowed Red to expand from the country market into the supermarket.

Red's Sauce launched in SuperValu in Westport and Castlebar in December 2012. He also sells in McCambridge's in Galway. Sales are up and busy, and Red reports that tastings get a great response. I'm not surprised.

Useful Resources
- County Dublin Beekeepers' Association (**www.dublinbees.org**);
- Grow It Yourself (GIY) (**www.giyinternational.org**);
- Quickcrop (**www.quickcrop.ie**);
- The Federation of Irish Beekeepers' Associations (**www.irishbeekeeping.ie**).

12

DUCK EGGS

Introduction

Duck eggs fell out of fashion just after World War II, when a health scare connected eating duck eggs with outbreaks of salmonella poisoning. Whatever the reason, demand for duck eggs plummeted and the mass producers ignored ducks in favour of the more easily farmed chicken.

Later, the large-scale farming methods involved in chicken egg production took control of the whole egg market. Chicken eggs were cheaper and more convenient. While duck eggs are not very widely available still, they can be found in some farm shops, delis, whole food shops, farmers' markets and so on – and there is considerable anecdotal evidence of unregistered eggs being sold in local shops, under the counter (including in a hairdressers!).

A duck egg can be used as a direct substitute for a normal hen's egg. The yolks are larger and higher in fat than a hen's egg, which makes them richer and perhaps a little 'gamey'. They also are packed with vitamins and minerals, and provide a powerful protein boost, approximately 15% of the adult recommended daily allowance. In baking, duck eggs work really well and many home bakers use them in preference to hen eggs.

There also has been an increase in the popularity of duck eggs for eating. As a result, there is an opportunity for new and existing duck egg producers to meet this market demand.

History

In 2010, there was a major outbreak of *Salmonellosis* in Ireland, which was associated with the consumption of undercooked duck eggs or consumption of raw foods made with duck eggs. The problem was that, up until this time, there were few if any controls in place for duck egg production and control.

However, subsequently, control measures have been implemented by the Department of Agriculture, Food and the Marine (DAFM) and the Food Safety Authority of Ireland (FSAI) in order to attempt to restore consumer confidence. The FSAI issued a factsheet – *Salmonella spp. and Eggs: Food Safety Advice for Caterers* – in order to provide some guidance. It is available on the FSAI website (**www.fsai.ie**).

DAFM has produced a code of practice for producers of duck eggs intended for sale in retail premises. This includes sourcing of flocks from a registered operator, implementing a salmonella monitoring programme and stamping of eggs with a producer code to provide traceability. For more information, including legislation controlling duck eggs, see **www.agriculture.gov.ie**.

In a parliamentary question in May 1949, then Minister for Agriculture, Mr. Dillon, was asked:

> "... whether he is aware that serious financial loss is caused to egg producers and exporters because of the fact that there is no sure market for duck eggs ...".

In response, the Minister replied:

> "Duck eggs have not been exported from this country since 1941 and, as producers have been aware for nearly nine years that there is no outlet for such eggs except on the home market".

Not much has changed since 1949. At the present time, few if any duck eggs are exported. However, the home market has increased in recent years. While most sales to date have been from backyard producers selling at farmers' markets or from the farm gate, on-going improvements in production and control standards will help to generate customer trust and so bring duck eggs back into popularity.

Duck Egg *vs* Hen Egg

Farm-fresh free range duck eggs and hen eggs are similar in both appearance and flavour. The yolks are deep orange, the flavour is rich and the eggs 'stand-up' when placed into a frying pan. Farm-fresh eggs also 'stay together' when dropped into hot water while being poached.

A significant health benefit claimed for duck eggs is that some people who have an allergic reaction to hen eggs are able to eat duck eggs without any adverse reaction, though I've only got anecdotal evidence for this, no hard scientific fact.

Duck eggs have more albumen (protein in the egg white) than a chicken egg. Fans of duck eggs say that scrambled eggs and omelettes are richer in flavour. Duck eggs are especially useful in baking, given the higher proportion of yolk to white – bakers report that the additional protein gives cakes and buns more 'lift'.

While duck eggs can be used in the same way as hen eggs when baking or cooking, the baker will need to do some calculations to take the difference in size and weight into account. The average weight of a duck egg is approximately 80 grams, while an average hen egg is about 50 grams. Care should be taken not to overcook duck eggs, as their higher water content tends to make them rubbery. The shells of duck eggs are thicker than hen eggs, which generally gives them a longer shelf life.

Best Breeds for Duck Egg Production

The breed most commonly used for egg production is the Khaki Campbell, a medium-sized brown duck that should have a flock life of three to four years. It produces on average 300 eggs per year, provided that proper management and feeding are carried out. Khaki Campbells are very active with a sturdy and upright posture. They are extremely hardy and are at home on land as well as water.

The Pekin breed of duck will lay between 150 and 180 eggs per year.

The Chiltern Duck is a hybrid duck, often confused with the Aylesbury. Chilterns are specially bred for laying, laying 350 slightly off-white-tinted eggs per year that are larger on average than Khaki Campbells. The ducklings are very fast growers, easily reared and hardy.

The Aylesbury duck is primarily a meat duck, producing excellent meat and in excess of 100 eggs per year. The Aylesbury duck is an old duck and, in some parts, a rare breed but it was one of the main meat-producing ducks kept by smallholders in large quantities up until WWII. It is a very good duck for the smallholder and home producer to keep. It will reach up to 10lb in weight (some times more) at around nine weeks but to obtain this, the ducks must be fed a high quality grain diet, otherwise their maximum weight will take many weeks longer.

Khaki Campbell

Pekin

Indian Runner

© www.freerangepoultry.ie

© www.freerangepoultry.ie

© gynti_46 / Flickr Creative Commons

Another good egg producer is the Indian Runner, which can produce over 250 eggs per year.

Note that ducks are social animals and need the company of other ducks; they do not keep very well as solitary birds.

General Requirements

DAFM publishes useful *Guidelines for Producers of Small Quantities of Duck Eggs (Backyard Flocks)*, which is available from the website (**www.agriculture.gov.ie**).

Ducks need a dry solid duck house/coop for sleep and shelter, as well as fresh clean grass. Ducks are at risk of predators so a predator-proof enclosure would be useful, though not everyone is able to provide one, and many duck farmers prefer their birds to roam free in the field. Unlike hens, ducks must have a pond or pool of fresh, clean, regularly-changed water to refresh themselves. The water must deep enough for them to submerge their whole head, which they need to do in order to keep their eyes moist.

The site should be clearly secured at all times to prevent any entry of unauthorised personnel or vehicles that might bring in infection. Salmonella can spread from ducks to other poultry species, animals and humans. The perimeter of the site should be clearly identified and, if possible, fenced.

Ducks can be very messy as their droppings are wet, so regular cleaning of their housing is important. Also if they are confined to a small patch of ground, it is very important that the birds are moved regularly to fresh ground – otherwise problems will occur.

Duck Houses

Duck housing does not differ significantly from other poultry housing, except that ducks do not need perches. Artificial lighting must be provided to ensure all-year-round production (16 hours of light per day). Houses consist of a slatted area and a veranda or litter area. There must be dry litter on the floor of the building to absorb their wet droppings. This will need to be changed regularly to reduce any chance of disease.

Ducks need good size egg laying nests of at least 12" (300mm) square or preferably larger. These also need to be of sufficient depth – around 8" (200mm) lined with deep straw, which again will need to be changed regularly because ducks can come in wet from the outside.

The building can be made from anything as long as it is dry and it can be much lower in height than other poultry houses as ducks are ground-dwellers. In good weather, the ducks may not use the housing at all except to lay.

Clean, fresh drinking water must be available 24 hours a day and the drinking vessel must be deep enough for the ducks to submerge all of their beaks. Fresh drinking water should be changed at least twice daily.

Code of Practice

The *Code of Practice for Duck Table Egg Producers*, issued in 2010 by DAFM and available on **www.agriculture.gov.ie**, includes the general requirements for the rearing of point-of-lay ducks for the production of table eggs and the general requirements for egg production systems. Duck egg producers should seek advice from recognised sources and consult the relevant and current guidelines/publications produced by DAFM and other bodies.

Feeding Ducks

Ducks will eat almost anything and will consume a lot of grass and vegetation – even insects. In fact, some are prolific slug-eaters, so they become the gardener's friend. As they have access to clean, free-ranging, fresh vegetation, farmers could make their own feed from crushed or rolled grain. Chicks require special chick crumb for the first six to eight weeks of their lives.

The Economics of Production

Building or conversions for providing duck houses will be the greatest part of the investment cost.

For small-scale production, supplying farm-gate sales or farmers' markets, the upgrading of an existing bird house is the most cost-effective option. Larger production units require state-of-the-art facilities and the construction of a purpose-built house. Equipment needed for the flock includes feeders, drinkers, nest boxes and slats. Somewhere to store feed is needed, as is fencing. Automatic drinkers are essential regardless of flock size, while other equipment choice will be governed by flock size.

Requirement for investment capital depends on where you are starting from, how many ducks you plan to have and whether everything will be done by hand or if you plan to have some automation. Teagasc advises that assessment of needs and costs is typically carried out on a case-by-case basis, and so calculating costs is not standard.

As a guide, birds may cost between €3 and €9 each. Websites such as Done Deal (**www.donedeal.ie**) list many suppliers, but it is essential that birds are purchased only from a registered, reliable source. Registration fees are €100 to DAFM, with a further €100 to Bord Bia likely in the future when the Egg Quality Assurance Scheme (EQAS) for hen eggs is extended to duck eggs. Other costs include testing fees for water and faecal samples. You might expect the following output volumes (eggs/year):

	Total per annum/bird	Packs/bird @ 6/box
Khaki Campbell	300	50
Indian Runner	250	41
Pekin	180	30
Aylesbury	100	16
Chiltern	350	58

Eggs typically sell for between €2.20 and €3.99 for six, depending on the shop. For example, according to *The Irish Times'* Reader's Forum (12 September 2011): "Fallon & Byrne, Exchequer St., Dublin - €3.99 for six free range duck eggs. Asia Market on Drury Street. ... free range duck eggs from the same farm, same sell-by date ... €2.50. Avoca were selling the duck eggs for €3.99, ... some butchers selling them for €3.50". The shop will add on its margin, so unless you are selling direct to consumer then remember the retail price is not the price you will get. So, your income, based on 100 birds, might be:

Breed	Number of Packs @ 6 eggs /box	Sell to shop for €2/box €	Gross Annual income (100 birds)* €
Khaki Campbell	50	100	10,000
Indian Runner	41	82	8,200
Pekin	30	60	6,000
Aylesbury	16	32	3,200
Chiltern	58	116	11,600

* *This calculation does not take into account the costs of housing, feed, testing, transport, packaging, etc.*

Value-added

The potential for adding value to duck eggs is limited. However, salted duck eggs are popular on the Asian market. Demand for duck eggs may be led by the Chinese and Asian communities, and so producers should consider looking at these markets.

The practice of salting duck eggs may have started as a method of preservation, but salted duck eggs are now considered a delicacy. Salting makes the egg whites dense and almost rubbery in appearance, but it is the yolk that is especially prized. If properly salted, the duck egg yolks are creamy, granular, and oily all at once – an unusual texture that tastes especially rich and salty.

Salted duck eggs are available ready-salted, cooked, and vacuum-packed at many Chinese or specialist grocery stores.

Future Developments

The regularisation of duck egg production will benefit all producers, as some backyard producers have brought duck eggs into disrepute in recent years. Duck egg producers require support as changing from old methods to new documentation and procedures will pose a challenge to many.

Legislation and Food Safety

Registration

All flocks, including backyard flocks, must be registered with DAFM. You will find application forms available for download on **www.agriculture.gov.ie**; when completed, these should be returned to the local District Veterinary Office.

In July 2011, DAFM emphasised the need for anyone who keeps poultry, who deals or trades in poultry, including anyone who keep small numbers of poultry for their own use, to register with the Department. The purpose of registration, which is a relatively easy process, is simply to ensure that DAFM has a full picture of where poultry are located, so that it can alert owners quickly in the event of a disease outbreak and also give advice on appropriate precautionary, containment and control measures as soon as possible.

Food Safety Authority of Ireland

FSAI publishes a factsheet – *Salmonella spp. and Eggs Food Safety Advice for Caterers* – which can be found on **www.fsai.ie**, under Resources and Publications. Issue 1, May 2010 gives advice for the safe usage of duck eggs:

- Duck eggs should not be eaten raw;
- Only eat duck eggs that have been thoroughly cooked, until both the white and yolk are solid;
- If you are preparing a dish that contains duck eggs, ensure that you have cooked it thoroughly before eating it;
- Do not use raw duck eggs in the preparation of products that contain raw or lightly cooked egg, such as homemade mayonnaise, tiramisu, icing or hollandaise sauce;
- When using duck eggs in cooking or baking, do not eat or taste the raw mix;

- After handling raw duck eggs, always wash your hands thoroughly;
- Ensure all utensils and preparation surfaces that have been in contact with raw duck eggs are washed thoroughly before being re-used;
- Store duck eggs in the fridge away from ready-to-eat foods.

Bord Bia Egg Quality Assurance Scheme

The Egg Quality Assurance Scheme (EQAS) in place for hen eggs does not currently apply to duck eggs; therefore, duck eggs cannot carry the quality assurance logo. Duck eggs are not included in the egg marketing regulations either and therefore they do not have to carry markings on the egg itself to indicate the Best Before date or traceability information. However, this information should be included on the packaging, or on the accompanying documentation if there is no packaging.

While duck eggs are not covered by the EQAS, it is recommended that producers should work towards these requirements, as any revision of the standard in future may include duck eggs.

Labelling

Packaging should include instructions to cook duck eggs thoroughly. It is recommended that boxes/packs of duck eggs should be labelled similarly to hen eggs. Eggs sold in boxes/packs therefore should have the following displayed on the packaging:

- **Name, address and identification number (approval number) of the packing centre:** You will get this once you register with DAFM;
- **Best Before date:** Use an ink stamp that you can apply by hand;
- Number of eggs in the pack;
- Advice to consumers to keep eggs refrigerated after purchase.

Where eggs are not sold in packs, retailers are required to display labelling information with each batch of eggs. As noted above, this labelling must be clearly visible to the customer and should include:

- Identification number (approval number) of the packing centre;
- Best Before date;
- Advice to consumers to keep eggs refrigerated after purchase;
- An indication of farming method used.

Note: A batch is defined as "eggs from the same source with the same Best Before date and the same quality and weight grading".

Table hen eggs marketed in the EU must be graded by quality and weight and be packed, labelled, stored, transported and presented for sale in conformity with EU and national legislation on the marketing standards for eggs. No similar scheme is currently in place for duck eggs, though producers are encouraged to comply with the general requirements as best practice.

If you are not sure what labelling information to put on the eggs or boxes, just ask your local DAFM inspector who you will get to know once you register with them.

Distribution and Marketing

Eggs are highly perishable with a short shelf life. So it is absolutely essential that you identify your market and customers before committing to setting up a duck egg venture. While this may not be as important for other areas of new business development, it is absolutely essential for perishable poultry and eggs.

The production and marketing of duck eggs is financially viable only when you can charge more for them than readily-available/mass-produced hen eggs.

Where Can I Sell Duck Eggs?

Farm-produced duck eggs may be sold door-to-door, from the farm-gate or at farmers'/country markets at present without having to date-mark or stamp the eggs. However, eggs **may not** be sold through shops or other outlets unless they are date-marked/stamped appropriately.

Who Is My Market?

Bakers consider duck eggs to function better than hen eggs, and home bakers in particular often favour them. Demand for duck eggs is strong in Chinese and Asian communities, where salted duck eggs and other delicacies are popular, and so producers should consider addressing this particular ethnic market.

Case Studies

Bernie Quinn Duck Eggs

Bernie Quinn has 120 free range ducks on her farm outside Ballyhaunis, Co. Mayo, where she has been operating since 1991. She is registered and approved with DAFM and currently supplies several shops and supermarkets in Ballyhaunis, Kiltimagh, Claremorris, Cloonfad, Swinford, Castlerea, Foxford, Castlebar and Ballina.

Parkview Farm

Parkview Farm is a family-run business in Tourlestrane, South Sligo, producing free range duck eggs (**www.parkviewduckfarm.com**). The business was established in 2009 by the Mulgrew family, who personally tend their flock of over 800 ducks. The

ducks are bedded on fresh clean straw at night-time.

Glenfin Farm

Brian Phelan is the owner-manager of Glenfin Farm (**www.glenfinfarm.ie**), a business based in Co. Monaghan that has become a leading distributor of award-winning duck eggs in Ireland. Brian set up the business in 2008, now has a total of 2,500 ducks, with each one producing an egg a day. With two vans, he works with distributors to supply his eggs to specialist food stores and butcher shops around the country. One of Glenfin Farm's biggest customers is Avoca. In 2009, Brian Phelan was the Young Entrepreneur Award Winner at the annual JFC Innovation Awards.

Useful Resources

- Department of Agriculture, Food and the Marine, Pigmeat and Poultry Section:
  - **www.agriculture.gov.iefarmingsectors/poultry** has information/forms available to download;
  - Local advisors and offices are located all around the country;
- Teagasc has a poultry advisor (**www.teagasc.ie**);
- Bord Bia (**www.bordbia.ie**);
- Food Safety Authority of Ireland (**www.fsai.ie**);
- Irish Farmers Association (**www.ifa.ie**):
  - Alo Mohan, Chairman of National Poultry Committee, (087) 629 2456;
  - Amii Cahill, Executive Secretary of National Poultry Committee, (01) 450 0266;
- Useful websites:
  - Irish Fowl: Includes a Directory of Irish poultry breeders (though not exhaustive) (**www.irishfowl.com**);
  - Irish-Poultry.com: Includes list of upcoming poultry sales and shows in Ireland (**www.irish-poultry.com**);
  - Poultry Ireland: Good general resource with links to other sites, events listing (**www.poultry.ie**);
  - *Practical Poultry* magazine (**www.practicalpoultry.co.uk**);
  - Rainbow Free Range Poultry (**www.freerangepoultry.ie**);
- Suppliers:
  - Billy Bob's Pet & Country Superstore: Poultry equipment and housing (**www.billybobs.ie**);
  - Connacht Gold: Full range of agri-supplies (**www.connachtgold.ie**);

o   Farm supply stores and co-ops listed in *Golden Pages* or local
    newspapers;

o   Local poultry clubs: Great for support and information;

o   MacEoin Poultry Supplies Ltd (**www.maceoinltd.com**);

o   Old McDonald's Farm & Feed Store: Egg boxes and
    stamping kits (**www.oldmcdonald.ie**);

o   Straw Chip: housing and bedding.

13

ICE CREAM, YOGURT AND CHEESE

Introduction

Here we look at how you might go about developing a range of dairy products – for example, farmhouse or home-made cheese, ice cream and yogurt. Some other products are mentioned also though not in detail, such as country butter and bottled milk.

As with all food, the main force driving the market for dairy products comes from consumers. The development of dairy products is relevant to both dairy farmers and non-farming producers.

Farmhouse Cheese

Farmhouse cheese-making virtually died out in Ireland until the late 1970s. For at least 25 years before then, cheese-making in Ireland had been confined almost exclusively to large-scale factory production, mainly concentrating on cheddar production and mainly owned by the big dairy co-ops. However, today Ireland produces more farmhouse cheese varieties *per capita* than any other country in the world, according to the National Dairy Council. The production of quality Irish farmhouse cheese has expanded to the extent that there are over 30 members of Cáis, the Association of Irish Farmhouse Cheese-makers (**www.irishcheese.ie**).

The story about the cheese – its provenance – is of particular importance when branding and marketing cheese. Irish cheeses are associated not only with where they are made but also often with the individual cheese-makers themselves. Traceability of Irish farmhouse cheese can extend not just to a region or townland, but also often to a family.

The Opportunity

The majority of cheese producers in Ireland are in the South of the country. There are fewer cheese producers in Ireland north of the Galway-Dublin line, with Andrew Pelham Burn of Carrowholly in Westport, Marion Roeleweld of Killeen Farmhouse Cheese (**www.killeencheese.ie**) in Galway, Silke Croppe of Corleggy Cheeses (**www.corleggycheeses.com**) in Cavan and Glyde Farm (Bellingham Blue cheese – **www.bellingham.ie**) in Louth being some exceptions.

Market and Distribution

The main market for farmhouse cheese is the island of Ireland, although some producers are exporting. As with any new food, it is essential to carry out market research in advance to determine what gaps there may be in the market, whether local or national.

Almost all supermarkets now have artisan cheeses in their main fridges, as do many smaller and specialist shops. Horgan's in Mitchelstown (**www.horgans.com**) is one of the largest countrywide distributors of specialist cheese. The Traditional Cheese Company (**www.traditionalcheese.ie**) currently sources and supplies BWG Foods' retail and wholesale brands (Spar, Eurospar, Mace and XL stores nationwide), the majority of which are produced in Ireland. Using a third party for your distribution comes at a cost, and most producers are inclined to do the distribution themselves initially.

The Bord Bia *Guide to Farmhouse Cheese,* which is available on **www.bordbia.ie**, also identifies opportunities for farmhouse cheese on the home and export markets.

Production

Teagasc has produced a useful *Farmhouse Cheese Factsheet* (**www.teagasc.ie/publications** and filter for "Food"), which gives some facts and figures and describes the general production methods. Note that quark and soft cheeses are considerably easier to make compared to hard cheese varieties.

According to Eddie O'Neill, author of the Teagasc *Factsheet*, what you need are:

- Suitable premises, approved by the HSE/EHO;
- A stainless steel vessel where milk can be converted into cheese;
- A moulding/pressing area where the curds are formed into their final shape;
- A brine tank (most cheeses) to salt the cheese;
- A ripening room where the cheese is held under the right conditions of temperature and humidity;
- A packaging area where the cheese is weighed and packed prior to distribution;
- A cold room or refrigerator to store the packaged product.

Set-up Costs

Set-up costs include the price of the equipment, premises and/or conversion of existing building. You may have an existing building on your property, such as your garage or an old barn or outhouse, that could be converted into cheese making units. It is extremely difficult to give figures for costs where the conversion of existing buildings is required, as the work required will vary from one premises to another, depending on its state of repair. Whether a new premises or conversion, the costs of ensuring that the buildings meet hygiene regulations could be high. Advice on conversion and costings can be given on an individual basis by Teagasc, DAFM or your EHO.

The range of equipment needed can cost anything between €10,000 and €30,000. Some equipment suppliers are listed at the end of this chapter.

Running Costs

The main direct costs involved are milk, ingredients, electricity, packaging and labour. It takes about 10 litres of milk to make 1kg of cheddar cheese. Rennet costs typically €3 to €4 per 50ml. It is important that producers cost their own time into any business plan/cost calculations, as the labour input can be high.

The cost of marketing and distribution is extra, and distribution costs in particular can affect the overall viability of the business.

How Is Cheese Made?

Every cheese-maker has their own little secrets about their recipe and what they do at each step to distinguish their cheese from the others. Take a look at *The Craft of Cheese-making* on **www.bordbia.ie**. There are over 500 varieties of cheese recognised by the International Dairy Federation and over 1,000 in a 2011 study. The more moisture there is in the cheese, the softer it will be.

The diagram below gives a general overview of cheese-making:

Pour milk into a vat or container

⬇

Add starter culture to ripen the milk

⬇

Add rennet to produce curds and whey

⬇

Separate the curds from the whey

⬇

Press the curds into moulds

⬇

Turn the moulds to form the shape and release more whey

⬇

Apply pressure if a hard cheese is being made

⬇

Add salt, if required

⬇

Leave it to ripen (if desired)

⬇

Pack and label

⬇

Off to the shops!

Ripened cheese must be kept for a certain length of time, at a particular temperature and with certain other conditions to produce the quality and flavour desired. Some examples include Cheddar, Gruyère and Parmigiano Reggiano.

Return on Investment

The price you can sell your cheese for will vary depending on whether it is a speciality cheese and how far you are away from your market. The period from production to time of sale could be up to six months, so being realistic, it is highly likely that producers will have a negative cash flow in their first year.

Current Trends and Future Developments

Irish specialist cheeses have an international reputation for flavour and quality. Goat's cheese is now commonplace.

There are a few cheese-makers who use raw milk in the production of their cheeses. Caution is key when it comes to working with raw milk, and it is best to follow advice. A very high level of hygiene management is critical to ensure food safety when using raw milk, as raw milk may contain disease-causing bacteria. FSAI has issued a leaflet to this effect: *Health Risks from Unpasteurised Milk, 2009*, which is available to download on **www.fsai.ie**.

Farmhouse or Home-made Ice Cream

Ice cream is made by freezing and aerating a mixture of ingredients including milk, sugar, flavours and water. The composition of ice cream varies, but is usually about 12% milk fat, 11% non-fat milk solids, 15% sugar and the rest of the ingredients plus water accounting for the balance.

For farmhouse or home-made ice cream producers, provenance again plays an important role in marketing the product, with the name of the farm, locality or producer often the main focus of the brand.

History

It seems that everyone from the Chinese to the Italians and Americans lay claim to having invented ice cream!

In China, during the Tang period (AD 618-907), buffalo, cows' and goats' milk was heated and allowed to ferment. This 'yogurt' was then mixed with flour for thickening and camphor for flavour and was chilled before being served. King Tang of Shang apparently had a staff of 2,271 people, which included 94 ice-men!

Italian *gelato* dates back to the 16th century. Most stories give the credit to Bernardo Buontalenti, a native of Florence, Italy, who delighted the court of Catherina de Medici with his creation. Italians are certainly credited with introducing gelato to the rest of Europe, with Sicilian-born Francesco Procopio dei Coltelli being one of the most influential individuals in the history of gelato – being one of the first to sell it to the public.

In 1843, an American housewife Nancy Johnson invented the hand-cranked ice cream churn. She patented her invention and sold the patent for $200 to a Philadelphia kitchen wholesaler which, by 1847, made enough freezers to satisfy the high demand. From 1847 to 1877, more than 70 improvements to ice cream churns were patented.

The Market

The market for speciality ice creams is generally limited to local or regional for small producers and there are several farmhouse-type producers in Ireland at present. The premium or luxury end of the market has grown over the years and Bord Bia's research indicates that this trend seems set to continue.

While there are several artisan producers in the country, they seem to be concentrated in the South and East, with just a few in the West/ North West. This may represent an opportunity for a new artisan producer in those regions, concentrating on local/provincial distribution.

Opportunity

Ireland has the third highest consumption of ice cream *per capita* in Europe, with a retail market value of €75.8m, according to market research published by Bord Bia. The ice cream sector has been badly affected by the recession as have many other luxury or 'special treat' foods. But, if staying in is the new going out, then good quality ice cream will always be in demand as an indulgence, even if the consumer doesn't buy it just as often as they might have previously.

Consumers usually assume luxury ice cream will be full fat, but it is worthwhile trying to develop reduced fat versions in your range.

Interesting new flavours are a good way to get the consumer's attention – for example, Cinnamon & Cashew, Black Tea, Lemon Curd or Sweet Potato even! Gin & Tonic flavour is another one that caught my attention recently!

For Irish ice cream makers, there are also opportunities to target consumers who want allergen-free products, and children of course.

Production Method

You can buy ice cream machines ranging from 1 litre in size up to commercial scale, depending on how big a batch you want to make. You can start by hand and then move on to at least a partial batch manufacturing process. The recipe is a matter of trial and error. To use fresh fruit or liquid flavours? To add egg or not? And you will have to play around with the best method to give you the flavour and consistency you want.

Teagasc's *Ice Cream Factsheet* (**www.teagasc.ie/publications** and then filter for "Food") gives some facts and figures and describes the general commercial production method.

As for all food products, you will need premises that meet the EU hygiene legislation, and you must notify your local EHO. If you are farm-based, then contact your local DAFM office.

For ice cream production, you need a processing area, a cold room and a freezer room, an area to store dry ingredients and an area to store packaging. Equipment for processing ranges in price enormously and can be quite expensive.

Farmhouse Yogurt

Yogurt has been a vital form of calcium in the diet in South Eastern Europe and Asia Minor for thousands of years. However, it was largely unknown outside these communities until scientific research suggested a direct link between yogurt and the unusually long lifespan enjoyed by Bulgarian peasants. Though this link was never proven, yogurt quickly gained popularity across Europe and the USA, particularly after fruit was added to improve the flavour and it began to be produced commercially.

The National Dairy Council (**www.ndc.ie**) says that yogurt was introduced into the Irish dairy market in the 1970s and soon became a household essential, particularly popular with younger consumers.

The Market
Adults eat the most yogurt, about half of the total market, followed by yogurt drinks and then children's yogurt.

Opportunity
While there are very many large commercial producers in the market, consumers are always interested in something new and locally-made, and are prepared to pay for it. Shoppers see yogurt as an everyday standard purchase; it's not a luxury item generally (though it could be!). Any new producer should consider their target market, branding and USP, particularly if they are to try to compete with the big manufacturers.

Production Method (Small Batch)
Yogurt is produced by the bacterial fermentation of milk. The bacteria used to make yogurt are called 'yogurt culture'. Fermentation of the lactose in the milk by these bacteria produces lactic acid, which acts on the milk protein to give yogurt its texture and its characteristic flavour. So now you know!

There are two main types of yogurt: set and stirred. Set yogurt results when the incubation/fermentation of the milk takes place in the final container/packaging in which it is sold. Stirred yogurt, however, is produced after fermentation has been carried out in bulk, prior to final cooling and packaging.

You can make either plain or natural yogurt, fruit yogurt (by adding fruit and sweeteners) or flavoured yogurt (synthetic flavours and colours).

Frozen yogurt is made in the same way as for the more common refrigerated kind, but it is then deep-frozen to -20°C (and it might need more sugar and stabiliser to withstand the freezer temperatures).

The yogurt culture is usually made up of *Lactobacillus* and *Streptococcus* bacteria. However, you don't have to start growing the bacteria yourself (!), as commercially-produced yogurt itself is a convenient source of starter bacteria. Generally, a mixture of *Streptococcus* and *Lactobacillus* has been used to produce the yogurt and are still present in the starter.

The milk is first heated to 90°C to kill any undesirable bacteria and to denature the milk proteins so that they set together rather than form curds. The milk is then cooled to about 40 to 43°C for incubation (or you can cool it completely and reheat it later). The bacteria culture is then added, and the temperature is maintained for four to seven hours to allow fermentation. If you are adding fruit or flavours, add them after fermentation. Altogether, preparation time for a small batch at home in your kitchen can take six to eight hours (or overnight). You can find recipes and procedures for making yogurt in recipe books and elsewhere. Of course, you can buy a yogurt-making machine too!

The ingredients for a typical 500g batch of plain yogurt are:

- 500ml whole pasteurised milk;
- 25g dried milk powder (optional);
- 3 tbsp (75g) live, plain whole-milk yogurt – *starter culture*.

The ingredients costs for this 500g batch are:

	€
Milk (a litre of milk costs around €0.30 if buying direct from farm or €1.20 from a shop)	0.15 / 0.60
Good plain yogurt costs about €0.50/100g, 75g required as starter culture	€0.375
Total cost for ingredients per 500g batch	**€0.525 / 0.975**

Specific Food Safety Issues and Legislation

It is necessary for dairy producers to be registered with DAFM's Milk Policy Division. Existing milk producers can convert some of their quota into 'direct sellers quota', whilst non-milk producers of dairy products must make arrangements with DAFM to acquire quota.

Registration

The following information was obtained from the DAFM's Dairy Division, which is responsible for FBOs processing milk or manufacturing dairy products.

Anyone who wants to make a dairy product or process milk for direct human consumption must contact the Dairy Hygiene Division within DAFM in the first instance. An information pack is issued to the potential producer. This pack includes a letter outlining what is involved in the approval/registration process, relevant application form, copies of the relevant legislation, FSAI *Guidebook for New Artisan Producers*, Milk Quota FAQ (this only applies to cows' milk producers), TB Control Plan (goats' milk producers only), list of suppliers (goats' milk and also raw cows' milk).

Drinking Milk Plants

DAFM's Veterinary Public Health Inspection Service (VPHIS) supervises all drinking milk plants. If a FBO proposes to process **pasteurised** cows'/goats' milk for direct human consumption, they must complete an application form. This application form must be accompanied by plans, Standard Operating Procedures, HACCPs, etc. (This applies to drinking milk premises only. Note: A TB control plan must be provided for goats' milk suppliers/processors of goats' drinking milk.) VPHIS will advise the Dairy Hygiene Division as to the adequacy of the proposal put forward by the applicant.

Dairy Product Plants

DAFM's Dairy Controls and Certification Division (DCCD) supervises anyone involved in the production of dairy products, including cheese-cutting/packing plants. The producers must complete and submit an application form. If the milk is used to manufacture a raw cows' milk product, the producer is obliged to inform DAFM from where s/he is sourcing the milk, as herds providing raw milk for the production of raw milk product are subject to two TB tests annually. DCCD notifies the local District Vet Office (DVO) as to who is supplying raw cows' milk in their area and the DVO schedules the testing (the list of raw cows' milk suppliers is reviewed annually by DCCD). In the event of a herd breakdown (due to TB), DCCD would carry out a risk assessment as to whether cheese would have to be recalled, destroyed or withheld from the market. If the producer is purchasing milk for the manufacture of dairy products direct from a farmer, then they must comply with the *Milk Quota Regulations* also (see below).

Goats' Milk Products

Application is made to the Dairy Hygiene Division in DAFM in the normal way. However, there is a bit more work involved with goats' milk suppliers/processors. DAFM does not have a compensation scheme in place for goat herds infected with TB. To minimise the risk of TB infection in goat herds, DAFM requires that every goats' milk supplier or processor using milk from their own herd must complete a TB control plan in respect of their herd, in conjunction with the herd owners' private veterinary practitioner, who also must sign, date and stamp the plan. The plan should outline the stock numbers, husbandry method and the testing frequency of the herd. The plan is then reviewed by DAFM and the herd owner is advised as to its adequacy. The Dairy Hygiene Division has advised all goats' milk processors currently in operation that they must not accept goats' milk from a supplier who has not provided them with a copy of their TB control plan that has been approved by DAFM. The processors also have been advised to request evidence from the supplier that the herd is TB free – for example, a copy of the herd's most recent test results. Similar to raw cows' milk, if a goat herd goes down with TB, the Dairy Hygiene Division will carry out a risk assessment on the case.

Raw Milk for Direct Human Consumption

DAFM is proposing to ban the sale of raw milk for direct human consumption. Legislation is at a very advanced stage and the ban is imminent. Although raw cows' milk has been banned since 1997, the new ban will include raw milk from all milking animals – for example, goats and sheep. This ban will not affect product made from raw milk, only drinking milk.

Purchasing Milk from an Approved Source

The following information in this section was obtained from the Meat and Milk Policy Division, DAFM (Dairy Hygiene Division).

In relation to a new entrant starting in production of ice cream, yogurt or cheese, there may be milk quota implications, depending on where the new entrant is sourcing the milk for their product. Bear in mind that the milk quota system will end in 2015 so there will be no restriction on the volume of milk produced and hopefully plenty of milk available as a result.

With a milk quota, a milk producer can produce milk up to their annual quota limit without fear of incurring a levy. If the milk producer produces over their quota, then they may incur a levy should the country as a whole also exceed the total available national quota in that quota year. A quota year runs from 1 April to 31 March.

A milk producer's quota can be assigned to one, or more than one, milk purchaser, who the producer then can supply. A milk purchaser is an entity that is registered to purchase milk from milk producers under the EU quota regulations.

A milk producer also can assign some, or all, of their available quota to 'direct sellers'. A direct seller is someone who sells, or supplies, their own milk, or milk-based products, directly to the consumer, rather than selling their milk to a registered milk purchaser. All milk produced for sale or supply must be accounted for under the quota regulations.

If the potential new entrant is not a milk producer themselves and needs to source their milk from somewhere else, they have two options available: purchase the milk from an existing milk purchaser, or purchase it directly from a milk producer. If they go with the first option and purchase milk from an existing milk purchaser, then there are no quota implications for them. The likes of Glanbia, Kerry, Dairygold, etc are all registered milk purchasers. The milk has been accounted for already under the quota regulations by the milk purchaser, so a new entrant buying their milk from an existing milk purchaser has no quota considerations to worry about.

If the new entrant decides to purchase the milk directly from a milk producer, then they themselves need to register as a milk purchaser through DAFM. Once registered as a milk purchaser, the new entrant would have to find a milk producer willing to transfer a portion of their available quota to them in order that they can commence supplying them (the new entrant).

A milk purchaser under the milk quota regulations has record-keeping and reporting obligations that they must put in place and maintain to satisfy the milk quota regulations. The records include the quantity of milk intake each year, the fat content of the milk they purchase, the butterfat adjusted milk intake figure, etc. Where such records are not maintained or reported to DAFM, a milk purchaser may be de-registered and may be guilty of an offence under the quota regulations, leading to a potential fine or imprisonment.

If a potential new entrant were themselves to be a milk producer and had sufficient quantities of milk available to them, then they could register as a direct seller with DAFM. As a direct seller, a milk producer would be able to produce some, or all, of their own milk for the purpose of sale or supply directly to the consumer.

Again, under the quota regulations, a direct seller has record-keeping and reporting obligations under the quota regulations similar to that of a milk purchaser. It is also possible that a direct seller would incur a 'super' levy if they were to produce milk for the purposes of direct sales over and above their available direct sales quota.

There is a large amount of both national and EU legislation surrounding all aspects of the milk quota regime such as European Commission *Regulation 595/2004*, Council *Regulation 1234/2007* and our own Statutory Instrument, *S.I. 227 of 2008*, in addition to any regulations governing the hygiene requirements.

If a person is considering becoming a new entrant to cheese, yogurt and ice cream production, then they are best advised to contact DAFM directly to discuss their own individual situation and to obtain full details of the requirements they would need to meet in starting up their enterprise.

Case Study – Cheese

For information on members of Cáis, the Association of Irish Farmhouse Cheese-makers, see the website **www.irishcheese.ie**.

Carrowholly Cheese

Carrowholly Cheese is a multi-award-winning Gouda-style farmhouse cheese made on the shores of Clew Bay on Ireland's scenic Atlantic coastline. It is made from raw cow's milk, collected from local farmers. Each cheese is made by hand by Andrew  Pelham Burn and production is kept intentionally small so as to ensure the outstanding quality of this cheese.

Case Study – Ice Cream

Murphy's Ice Cream

Sean and Kieran Murphy started Murphy's Ice Cream (**www.murphysicecream.ie**) in Dingle, Co. Kerry in 2000, with the goal of making the best ice cream in the world. Murphy's Ice Cream uses milk from the rare, indigenous breed of Kerry cow because the milk is so wonderful (*note the provenance!*).

Quality and originality are of primary importance – the brothers say that they never use preservatives, colours, mixes, powdered milk, bottled flavours, or anything not natural. They use Dingle sea water to boil down to make sea salt ice cream and fresh mint leaves for the fresh mint ice cream.

Having started out making ice cream in the back of their shop in Dingle, they have moved recently into bigger production premises. In their own words, "We now have bigger pots and pans, but we still make ice cream the same way – breaking eggs and using fresh cream, milk and pure cane sugar to make a delicious custard that we flavour with fresh, natural, real ingredients".

Some other well-known Irish ice cream producers include:
- Baldwin's Farmhouse Ice Cream, Waterford (**www.baldwinsicecream.com**);
- Featherbed Farm Luxury Ice Cream (**www.featherbedfarm.ie**);
- Glastry Farm Ice Cream, Co. Down (**www.glastryfarm.com**);
- Linnalla Ice Cream, Co. Clare (**www.linnallaicecream.ie**);
- Paganini Ice Cream, Wexford (**www.paganini.ie**);
- Rossmore Farmhouse Ice Cream, Co. Laois (**www.rossmorefarm.ie**);
- Silver Pail Dairy, Co. Cork (**www.silverpail.com**);
- Tipperary Organic Ice Cream (**www.tipperaryorganic.ie**);
- Valentia Island Farmhouse Dairy, Co. Kerry (**www.valentiadairy.com**).

Case Study – Yogurt

Kilbeg Dairies

Located in some of the most lush and fresh pasture of Co. Meath, Kieran and Jane Cassidy have developed award-winning dairy products from fat-free quark cheese to creamy rich mascarpone.

Jane, a former nurse, had always been passionate about food and returned from a Teagasc course knowing what she was destined to do. "The first time I made quark, I fell in love with the process, time, smells, flavours, textures and the concept of turning a simple natural ingredient such as milk into a myriad of delicious dairy products".

Beginning in her kitchen and selling at local markets, Kilbeg Dairies (**www.kilbegdairies.ie**) now produces a multi-award-winning range that has an authentic flavour and texture, due to the special blend of ingredients and techniques used. In response to customer demand, Kilbeg also has developed a delicious fat-free range to compliment the full fat range of products.

Some other producers include:

*   Glenilen Farm (**www.glenilenfarm.com**);
*   Glenisk yogurts and milk (**www.glenisk.com**);
*   Irish Yogurts in Clonakilty, West Cork (**www.irish-yogurts.ie**);
*   Killowen Farm Yogurt, at the foot of the Blackstairs Mountains, outside Courtnacuddy, Co. Wexford (**www.killowen.ie**).

Training Providers

Cheese-making

Courses for both soft and hard cheese-making are available from:

*   CAFRE (**www.cafre.ac.uk**);
*   Carrowholly Cheese;
*   Food Industry Training Unit, University College Cork (**www.ucc.ie/fitu**);

- Knockdrinna: A one-day cheese-making course where you make your own cheese in the morning, enjoy lunch and then take your handmade creation home for maturing. For those in the catering industry or interested food production for a living, Helen Finnegan is currently designing a professional cheese-making guidance course (**www.knockdrinna.com**);
- National Organic Training Skillnets, open to non-organic producers also (**www.nots.ie**);
- Producers offering training courses include Silke Croppe at Corleggy Cheeses (**www.corleggycheeses.com**);
- Teagasc, Moorepark Food Research Centre, Fermoy: Three-day course (**www.teagasc.ie**);
- The Organic Centre: Instructors: Hans and Gaby Wieland. Cost €155. Claims to be the only such course in the country covering all aspects of cheese-making including cultures, equipment and facilities. Butter-making courses also available (**www.theorganiccentre.ie**).

Ice Cream-making

Providers include:

- Alfred & Co.: Occasional one-day courses covering the basics of ice cream formulation and manufacturing, including presentations and 'hands on' sessions using items of equipment from their portfolio. Course content particularly useful for farm-based producers (**www.alfredandco.com**);
- CAFRE (**www.cafre.ac.uk**);
- Carpigiani UK Ltd: An Italian ice cream equipment manufacturer, providing high quality equipment and services, they run ice cream-making courses at *Gelato University* in Bologna and the UK (**www.carpigiani.co.uk**);
- Food Industry Training Unit, University College Cork: Ice Cream Science & Technology course (fee €1,200). This intensive three-day course provides participants with knowledge of the production,

science, technology, and quality features of frozen desserts, ice cream and related products (**www.ucc.ie/fitu**);

- RSS Ltd: The *Introduction to Artisan Ice Cream and Fruit Ice* course is suited to newcomers to the world of ice cream and gives a good overview of what is required to have your own ice cream business. RSS also organises a more advanced course with an Italian chef either in Italy or in Hereford, UK (**www.rsshereford.co.uk**);
- Servequip: Now running a one-day training course once a month, showcasing the latest equipment from Frigomat. This course also will keep you updated on all the latest industry ideas and trends (**www.servequip.co.uk**);
- The Ice Cream Alliance, through NOTS (**www.ice-cream.org**).

Yogurt-making

Providers here include:

- AB Cheesemaking (UK): Yogurt-making courses, cost £456.00, payable in full on application (**www.abcheesemaking.co.uk**);
- Ballymaloe Cookery School: Yogurt, butter and cheese-making (**www.cookingisfun.ie**);
- CAFRE (**www.cafre.ac.uk**);
- National Organic Training Skillnets: Yogurt and butter-making – €200 for three-day course (**www.nots.ie**);
- Society of Dairy Technology (**www.sdt.org**);
- The Organic Centre: Cheese and yogurt courses, prices approx. €140 (**www.theorganiccentre.ie**).

Equipment and Ingredients Suppliers

Note: Prices can vary from a few hundred € to up to €5k depending on size, make, capacity.

Cheese Equipment Suppliers

- ALPMA (UK): Specialists in equipment for cheese-making and packaging (**www.alpma.co.uk**);
- Jongia (**www.jongia.com**);

- Moorlands Cheesemakers (**www.cheesemaking.co.uk**);
- Old McDonald's Farm & Feed Store (**www.oldmcdonald.ie**);
- Rademaker BV (**www.rademaker.com**);
- Specialist Cheesemakers Association (**www.specialistcheesemakers.co.uk**);
- C. van't Riet Dairy Technology BV (**www.rietdairy.nl/?lid=2**).

If you are making a small amount of fresh cheese such as cottage- or curd-style cheese, natural live yogurt provides an ideal starter culture. You can also buy freeze-dried varieties.

The following companies offer a mail order service on cheese-making equipment:

- Fullwood Ltd. (**www.fullwood.com**);
- Goat Nutrition Ltd. (**www.gnltd.co.uk**);
- Moorlands Cheesemakers (**www.cheesemaking.co.uk**);
- Stratton Sales (USA) (**wwwstrattonsales.com**).

Yogurt Supplies

- Cloverhill Food Ingredients Ltd (**www.cloverhill.ie**);
- Old McDonald's Farm & Feed Store (**www.oldmcdonald.ie**)

Ice Cream-making Supplies

- Alfred & Co. (UK): Distributor of equipment from WCB Ice Cream, Technogel and Pancolini, covering brand names such as Crepaco, Glacier, Technohoy, Vitaline, PMS, Promco, Grafton and Anderson, all of whom are well regarded in the industry (**www.alfredandco.com**);
- Ashwood Trade Products (UK) (**www.ashwood.biz**);
- Cater Link (UK) (**www.caterlink.co.uk**);
- Dairyglen (**www.dairyglen.ie**);
- Martin Food Equipment (**www.martinfoodequip.com**);
- Nisbets: Supply both domestic and small commercial scale equipment (**www.nisbets.ie**).

Other Supplies

- *Buy & Sell* lists second hand equipment and ice cream carts for sale; and there are many commercial machines listed for sale on eBay (**www.buyandsell.ie**);
- Old McDonald's Farm & Feed Store (**www.oldmcdonald.ie**);
- Robot Coupe (**www.robotcoupe.co.uk**).

Useful Resources

- AB Cheesemaking (UK) (**www.abcheesemaking.co.uk**);
- Cáis, the Association of Irish Farmhouse Cheese-makers (**www.irishcheese.ie**);
- *Dairy Microbiology* by RK Robinson (1981) – an old text, but regarded as the definitive guide;
- DairyCo publication, *On-farm Small-scale Cheese-making: A Beginners Guide* (**www.dairyco.org.uk**);
- Department of Agriculture and Rural Development (NI), *Guide to Farmhouse Cheese Production*, available on **www.dardni.gov.uk**;
- Department of Agriculture, Fisheries and the Marine (**www.agriculture.gov.ie**);
- MakeIcecream.com;
- *Manufacturing Yogurt and Fermented Milks* by Ramesh C. Chandan, Blackwell Publishing;
- *Microbiology and Technology of Fermented Foods* by RK Hutchins (2006);
- Moorlands Cheesemakers (UK) (**www.cheesemaking.co.uk**);
- *On-farm Processing: A Beginners Guide*: Published in 2007 by the Milk Development Council (UK), it gives a broad point of reference for those considering the manufacture of their own dairy products and can be downloaded free from **www.dairyco.org.uk**;
- Slow Food Ireland: Irish Raw Milk Cheese Presidium (**www.slowfoodireland.com**);
- Society of Dairy Technology (**www.sdt.org**);

- Teagasc (**www.teagasc.ie**);
- The Cheese Hub: Offers cheese ripening and maturing facilities (**www.thecheesehub.ie**);
- The Cheese Web (**www.thecheeseweb.com**);
- The Ice Cream Alliance (UK) (**www.ice-cream.org**).

14

VALUE-ADDED MEATS

In this chapter we look at how best to approach the development of a range of value-added raw meats. The information is relevant for farmers producing livestock, butchers, who may or may not have their own supply of meat, and other producers of value-added meat products who are neither farmers nor butchers.

Consumer Trends

There is no doubt that consumers are turning back to more traditional-style meals with meat at the centre (with apologies to the vegetarian minority!). The appeal of everyday products that serve up a touch of premium is becoming more and more popular. An opportunity presents itself for butchers and producers of meat products to meet this demand.

There are a number of butchers producing good quality value-added meat products with several other pig, beef and lamb farmers producing some joints, but not adding value beyond that due to lack of skills and/or facilities.

Trends in the sector include meatballs, meal solutions (stuffed joint with raw vegetables in tray, straight to oven), smoked sausages and premium sausages (with at least 80% meat). Cornish pasties and old-fashioned meat pies are really making a comeback also! There is always a demand from consumers for good quality, locally-produced, value-added meat products that provide a 'meal solution'.

Working in co-operation with other producers can be very useful – for example, the local butcher supplying meat to local pasty-maker, who then sells their ready-to-cook pasties in the butcher's shop.

Selling value-added foods through butcher shops that have supplied the meat is a really good way to co-operate, each promoting the other.

Breed branding is becoming a more common feature, with breeds such as Angus and Wagyu (Kobe) becoming better known. Be sure to promote the breed of meat you are using, if it already has good brand recognition. Angus beef's association with quality is well-known and is positioned as a cut above 'ordinary' beef. Brands within retail and food service are increasingly playing on consumers' apparent growing appreciation of Angus beef.

The range of potential value-added products includes:

- Sausages;
- Burgers;
- Oven ready meals – stuffed joints with or without vegetables;
- Stir fries – with sauce and/or vegetables;
- Casserole mixes (with vegetables);
- Meatballs;
- Pasties.

How to Make Sausages

The production of value-added meat products has evolved from kitchen to butcher to factory. However, the quality of the meat, the key ingredient, is important in terms of producing flavour and eating quality.

Sausage Casings

The choice of sausage casings is between natural or synthetic.

Natural casings are more expensive and tricky to work with. Some natural casings are made from the intestines of the animal and are cleaned, bleached and preserved in salt and so these must be soaked in cold water before use (preferably overnight). Fresh casings have a shelf life of about two months if kept in salt and kept refrigerated. Fresh casings come on tapes or tubes so that they are easier to thread onto the filling nozzle. Natural casings are the only casings that can be used in organic sausage production.

Image source: **www.sausage-making.co.uk.**

Synthetic casings often are made from collagen and do not need any preparation and they are ready to use. They have a shelf life of about two years if stored correctly. They do not need to be refrigerated. Once these casings have been filled, it is important that the sausages are left in the refrigerator overnight to rest. The herbs and spices marinate with the meat and the skins rehydrate. These skins look and feel just like normal skins, and are often less 'chewy' than fresh casings.

Processing Partners

As the aim of the artisan producer is to sell value-added meat products to consumers, s/he needs access to or to partner with a butcher that can offer good quality cutting facilities.

Work with a local butcher who can offer a focussed service. You might not be able to afford to buy a sausage-making machine straight away, but perhaps your local friendly butcher would make the sausages for you, to your recipe, if you ask nicely!

Production Requirements

Producing raw or cooked meat products in the kitchen at home isn't really feasible. Meat products are considered to be high risk and there is no avoiding a dedicated place in which to prepare your foods.

If you are planning to make cooked meats, then you must have physically-separated raw and cooked areas. This is no small undertaking and should not be entered into lightly.

For raw meat products, what you will need is a combination of some or all of the following:

- Suitable dedicated premises, approved by your EHO or DAFM vet;
- Preparation area;
- Store for dry ingredients and for packaging;
- Sausage machine, mincing and mixing machines, knives and so on;
- A packaging area where the finished product is weighed and packed;
- A cold room to store the packaged product.

The capital costs of building and equipping a medium-sized facility (1,250 sq. ft.) might be as much as €100,000 if you are starting from scratch, not including the site. Conversion of an existing garage or other premises may be cheaper, though it depends on the conversion work that needs to be done. Equipment costs vary and are available from the suppliers listed at the end of this chapter.

Nonetheless, the word on the street is that margins on sausages are very high, and that they are a valuable product for butchers.

The Economics of Making Sausages

Let us look at the production of sausages, considering the various stages in the process separately to identify the costs and margins:

- **Supplier of raw materials:** Butcher;
- **Producer:** Sausage-maker;
- **Retailer:** Shop.

The butcher buys pigs for €25 per pig. Each results in 25kg of meat (€1/kg), which he sells for €2/kg.

Product	Direct Costs	Selling Price	Simple Gross Profit (SGP)	Simple Gross Margin (SGM)
	(1)	(2)	(3 = 2 − 1)	(4 = 3/2x100)
Meat	€1	€2	€1	50%

The sausage-maker makes 0.5kg of sausage from 1kg of meat, which he sells for €5. Labour cost is not included here, but all other ingredients cost €1.

Product	Direct Costs	Selling Price	SGP	SGM
	(1)	(2)	(3 = 2 − 1)	(4 = 3/2x100)
Sausages	€3	€5	€2	40%

The shop-owner sells the sausages for €9; his/her direct cost is the purchase price s/he paid the sausage-maker.

Product	Direct Costs	Selling Price	SGP	SGM
	(1)	(2)	(3 = 2 − 1)	(4=3/2x100)
Sausages	€5	€9	€4	44%

The Simple Gross Margin (SMG) in the chain shows:
- The butcher 50%;
- The processor 40%;
- The shop 44%.

Margins are highest for the butcher selling just meat, then the shop-owner who sells sausages and lowest for the sausage-maker.

However, if the butcher makes the sausages and sells them to the shop, the cost calculation changes as one of the middlemen is cut out.

Product	Direct Costs (1)	Selling Price (2)	SGP (3 = 2 – 1)	SGM (4 = 3/2x100)
Sausages	€2	€5	€3	60%

If the butcher makes and sells the sausages direct to the public, margins improve even further.

Product	Direct Costs (1)	Selling Price (2)	SGP (3 = 2 – 1)	SGM (4 = 3/2x100)
Sausages	€2	€9	€7	77%

In other words, the gross margins will change by either adding new functions or eliminating some functions:

- **The butcher buys pigs and sells meat to the sausage-maker:** SGM = 50%;
- **The butcher buys pigs, makes sausages and sells them to the shop:** SGM = 60%;
- **The butcher buys pigs, makes sausages and sells them direct to the public:** SGM = 77%.

This is how these results would look on a graph:

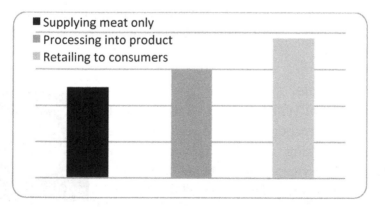

By presenting the margins in this way, you can see at a glance where the greatest margins (and so the best way to make the most money) lie. It shows how a producer can add value to meat.

Case Studies

The following value-added meat producers in Ireland are some good examples of the standards that can be achieved by small producers. Note how each has personalised their business and promotes tradition and provenance as a unique selling point (USP).

Coopershill Venison

Coopershill in Co. Sligo has been in the O'Hara family since it was built in 1774, with the 8th generation now calling it home. Approximately 250 fallow deer roam the fields at Coopershill and are grass-fed throughout spring and summer. Mother and son, the inimitable Lindy and Simon, encourage farm visits so that consumers of Coopershill Venison can see first-hand the importance that they attach to animal welfare (**www.coopershill.com/venison.html**).

The advantage of farmed over wild venison is that they know the exact age of each animal and therefore can guarantee flavour and tenderness of the meat. High in iron and a plethora of vitamins, very lean and low in saturated fat, venison is the perfect red meat for anyone who cares about their cholesterol levels but still enjoys an exquisite meal.

Irish Pasty People

Paul and Carmel Williams are a typical example of how people responded to the recession. Paul had been working as a draughtsman in an architectural services practice before he moved into the food business. He converted their garage himself, having contacted their local EHO early on and taking her advice, sourcing second-hand and refurbished equipment, and got started making high quality steak meat pasties (chopped not minced!) that he missed from his native England. Carmel became their Sales & Marketing person, calling to shops and securing sales across the region. They focus on food service, selling to hot food counters in supermarkets, school and corporate canteens.

Jack & Eddie's Sausages

The O'Malley family farm has been in existence for five generations. Jack is the fifth generation and Eddie, Jack's dad, is the fourth. The farm is nestled in the hills between Westport in Co. Mayo and Leenane, Co. Galway. Eddie is a farmer at heart but has always been concerned with the difficulty of making a living from farming. With many locals interested in tasting the produce, Eddie decided to start making sausages, which allows Eddie to continue to make a living from the farm (**www.jackandeddies.com**). Jack & Eddie use a secret family recipe for their sausages and a traditional cure for rashers from only the best cuts of pork.

Úna's Pies

With a Masters degree in Urban Planning & Sustainable Development from UCC, and a recession in Ireland, Úna Martin from Ballincollig, Co. Cork could not find employment and took a year out to travel South America and Australia. Her travels were cut short, however, when a business plan to start an artisan savoury pie company started brewing. Úna discovered that pies were huge in Australia but that there was nothing similar on the market in Ireland! Pies in Ireland had been associated with convenience, service station food with low meat content and lacking in flavour. She saw a gap in the market for an Australian-style gourmet pie company in Ireland and so, in 2011, Úna's Pies (**www.unaspies.ie**) was born.

Initially, Úna sold her pie creations at a local Country Market in Caherdaniel, Co. Kerry. The pies were well-received and it was soon time to think bigger. Over the next few months, Úna's Pies began to create a buzz at the Mahon Point and Douglas Farmers' markets in Cork. Devoted pie addicts tried and tested many a creation. Úna's Pies are ideal as a snack, lunch or with an accompaniment as dinner. With a high quality, high meat content, the pies are 100% traceable and handmade using the finest ingredients Ireland has to offer.

Since starting, Úna's Pies has received many awards, including the four at the 2011 Blas na hÉireann Irish Food Awards, five at the 2012 Blas na hÉireann Irish Food Awards, including Supreme Champion, and five Gold Stars at the 2013 Great Taste Awards. Úna's Pies are included in the Bridgestone Guide 2012. All of these awards are testament to the high quality ingredients sourced from local suppliers and the highly skilled pie production team at Úna's Pies.

Equipment Suppliers
- Brennan Group (**www.brennan-group.com**);
- *Buy & Sell* lists second hand equipment for sale (**www.buyandsell.ie**);
- Martin Food Equipment (**www.martinfoodequip.com**);
- McDonnell's Ltd (**www.mcdonnells.ie**);
- Nisbets: Supply both domestic and small commercial scale equipment (**www.nisbets.ie**);
- Old McDonald's Farm & Feed Store (**www.oldmcdonald.ie**);
- Robot Coupe (**www.robotcoupe.co.uk**);
- Scobie & Junor (Dublin) Ltd. (**www.scobiesdirect.com**).

Ingredient Suppliers
- Brennan Group (**www.brennan-group.com**);
- CaterPac: For packaging (**www.caterpac.ie**);
- CF Gaynor Ltd: For marinades, sauces, herbs and spices, sausage mixes and coatings (**www.cfgaynor.com**);
- Irish Casing Company Ltd: For casings (**www.irishcasings.com**);

- McDonnell's Ltd (**www.mcdonnells.ie**);
- Scobie & Junor (Dublin) Ltd. (**www.scobiesdirect.com**).

Useful Resources

General

- Campden BRI (UK) (**www.campden.co.uk**);
- Department of Agriculture, Food and the Marine (**www.agriculture.gov.ie**);
- Food Safety Authority of Ireland (**www.fsai.ie**);
- Leatherhead Food Research (UK) (**www.leatherheadfood.com**);
- Love Irish Food (**www.loveirishfood.ie**);
- Teagasc (**www.teagasc.ie**).

Training Providers

- Meat skills training:
  - CAFRE (**www.cafre.ac.uk**);
  - Dublin Institute of Technology, School of Culinary Arts & Food Technology: Sometimes runs courses in collaboration with the Associated Craft Butchers of Ireland (**www.dit.ie/culinaryartsandfoodtechnology/**);
  - Skillnets: Some Skillnets may have relevant courses (**www.skillnets.ie**);
  - Taste 4 Success Skillnet (**www.taste4success.ie**);
  - Butchery classes at James McGeough Butchers (**www.connemarafinefoods.ie**);
  - Butchery classes at James Whelan Butchers (**www.jameswhelanbutcher.com**);
- Teagasc: Butchery and meat management, food safety, labelling and more (**www.teagasc.ie**);

- Meat-specific courses:
  - o Andrew Chilton: Sausage-making course includes food safety; history of sausages; sausage-making process; recipes and practical sausage-making;
  - o Associated Craft Butchers of Ireland: Offers butchery training coupled with a recognised FETAC Level 5 qualification specific to butchery (**www.craftbutchers.ie**);
  - o Food Industry Training Unit, College of Science, Engineering and Food Science, University College Cork (**www.ucc.ie/fitu**);
  - o National Organic Training Skillnet (NOTS): Sausage-making courses; butchery and small scale meat production with Teagasc, Ashtown: Course covers the factors affecting the quality of meat; meat presentation / the potential uses of the various cuts of meat; labelling issues; handling of meat – food safety issues (**www.nots.ie**);
  - o Pat O'Doherty: Famous for his Black Bacon brand, also delivers training courses (**www.blackbacon.com**);
  - o Teagasc, Ashtown: Meat Hygiene, FETAC Level 5 – course covers animal welfare relating to slaughter; red meat slaughter procedure and hygiene controls; anatomy and physiology of farm animals; nutrition, growth and metabolism of farm animals; basic pathology and disease; post-mortem inspection procedures; food-borne illnesses and zoonoses; meat processing; the red meat industry – summary and future (**www.teagasc.ie**);
- Teagasc Food Research Centre, Ashtown in association with the Rural Food Skillnet:
  - o Introduction to Meat, Fish and Poultry Preparation and Management;
  - o Food Technology: Meat Technology (**www.teagasc.ie**).

15

SMOKED MEAT, CHEESE AND FISH

Introduction

If you plan to set up a smokehouse for producing smoked meat, cheese or fish, special consideration must be given to buying the unsmoked foods from a reliable source, obtaining the appropriate test results and ensuring that your supplier complies with all the relevant legislative and hygiene requirements.

Each of the three potential products in this chapter – smoked meat, cheese and fish – is addressed in terms of the market, the opportunity, equipment requirements, typical costs where available, marketing and distribution, and production method.

Cold Smoking

Cold smoking is one of the oldest known preservation methods. However, smoking of foods today is usually done for the flavour rather than for preservation. While the smoke is an anti-microbial and anti-oxidant, it is not sufficient for preserving food in practice, unless combined with another preservation method such as salt-curing or drying.

Cold smoking allows total smoke penetration into the side of the meat. Very little hardening of the outside surface of the meat (casing) occurs and smoke penetrates the meat easily. Cold smoking prevents or slows down the spoilage of fats, which increases their shelf life. Cold smoked products are not submitted to any heat and so are not cooked.

Some important points to remember:

- Cold smoking is carried out typically at temperatures between 10°C and 32°C;
- Only use containers that are made from either food grade plastic or high quality stainless steel for preparing meats;
- Don't use woods that have been treated, or come from an unknown source;
- Using dry wood is of utmost importance when cold smoking.

Smoked salmon is smoked with cold smoke for an extended period of time. Applying hotter smoke (over 28°C) will cook the fish – sometimes sold as 'barbequed salmon' – changing the flavour and making it more difficult to slice it as thinly as the cold smoked version.

Cold smoking is a slow process and hams, which lend themselves perfectly to this type of smoking, can be smoked from two to even six weeks. During smoking, they will slowly acquire a golden colour along with a smoky flavour.

Hot Smoking

Hot smoking dries out the surface of the meat, creating a barrier for smoke penetration. Although foods that have been hot smoked are often reheated or cooked, they are typically safe to eat without further cooking. Typical temperatures used are in the range of 52°C to 80°C.

Food Safety and Other Legislation

There are specific considerations to be taken into account when working with smoked fish. *Listeria monocytogenes* can survive at refrigeration temperatures and sometimes can be associated with food poisoning from smoked fish. The Sea Fisheries Protection Authority has produced a useful leaflet that can be downloaded from **www.sfpa.ie**. It is necessary for food producers who sell to the public to be registered with the HSE, as described already in **Chapter 3**.

Specific legislation applies to the use and declaration of smoke flavourings. The Environmental Protection Agency (**www.epa.ie**) advises that *Air Quality Regulations* for the smoke house may apply.

Case Studies

Smoked Cheese – Knockanore

Knockanore Farmhouse Cheese is manufactured from full cream cows' milk produced from the Lonergan Pedigree Friesian herd. It is then turned into wheels of cheese, some of which are carefully selected

and smoked, using a blend of oak hardwood in a traditional smoking kiln. The oak is locally sourced in the neighbouring heritage town of Lismore. This smoked cheese is available as a delicious full wheel or in pre-packed wedges. All of the cheeses are available also with a full range of herbs and spices (**www.knockanorecheese.com**).

Smoked Meat – Ummera Smokehouse

The vitality of fine quality food producers in the West Cork area helps the Ummera Smokehouse (**www.ummera.com**) to maintain a vibrancy and high level of interest, maintaining quality and continually developing expertise. Ummera smoked products (including smoked eel, smoked chicken, smoked duck and smoked dry cured bacon – with no artificial preservatives) are available at a range of outlets in Ireland, and also for direct sales from the smokehouse.

Smoked Fish – Burren Smokehouse

The award-winning Burren Smokehouse is a family-run artisan producer of smoked salmon products, set up in 1989 by Birgitta and Peter Curtin (**www.burrensmokehouse.ie**). The smokehouse supplies to high-end customers within the deli, restaurant and retail sector to customers worldwide. All the salmon is 100% Irish.

Smoked Foods Courses

- Food Industry Training Unit, College of Science, Engineering and Food Science, University College Cork (**www.ucc.ie/fitu**);

- National Organic Training Skillnet: Bacon-curing and smoking – one-day course on wet and dry curing and smoking (cost €80) (**www.nots.ie**);
- Old Smokehouse Foods & Equipment (UK) (**www.the-old-smokehouse.co.uk**);
- Smallholding Courses: Curing and smoking meat courses (**www.smallholdingcourses.co.uk**);
- Smoky Jo's Cooking School (UK) (**www.smokyjos.co.uk**).

Equipment Suppliers

Equipment can be purchased from a number of suppliers, who often offer training courses and can provide a great deal of technical and other advice. Prices can vary from a few hundred € to up to €5,000, depending on size, make, capacity, etc. Suppliers include:

- Macs BBQ (UK) (**www.macsbbq.co.uk**);
- Old McDonald's Farm & Feed Store (**www.oldmcdonald.ie**);
- Smoky Jo's Cooking School (UK) (**www.smokyjos.co.uk**).

16

WHERE TO NOW? HELP IS AT HAND

Many resources and sources of information have been mentioned throughout the book already. Here they are again, all in one place – along with a few more:

- **AB Cheesemaking**, 7 Daybell Close, Bottesford, Nottingham NG13 0DQ, www.abcheesemaking.co.uk, (01949) 842867 (00 44 prefix from RoI).
- **About Hygiene Ltd.**, Ballinamore, Co. Leitrim, www.about-hygiene.com, (071) 964 5111.
- **Alfred & Co.**, West Carr Road, Retford, Nottinghamshire DN22 7SN, www.alfredandco.com, info@icecream.alfred.co.uk, (01777) 701141 (00 44 prefix from RoI).
- **Algaran**, Cashling, Kilcar, Co. Donegal, www.algaran.ie / www.seaweedproducts.ie, rosaria@algaran.ie, (074) 973 8961.
- **Alpha Omega Consultants Ltd.**, Dromahair, Co. Leitrim, www.alphaomega.ie, oonagh@alphaomega.ie, (071) 916 4003.
- **ALPMA GB Ltd.**, 1 Devonshire Business Park, Knights Park Road, Basingstoke RG21 6XN, www.alpma.co.uk, info@alpma.co.uk, (01256) 467177 (00 44 prefix from RoI).
- **Andrew Chilton**, Boyle, Co. Roscommon, andrew.chilton@gmail.com, (086) 662 7415.
- **Andrews Food Ingredients**, 27 Ferguson Drive, Knockmore Hill Industrial Park, Lisburn, Co. Antrim BT28 2EX, www.andrewingredients.co.uk, leah@andrewingredients.co.uk, (028) 9267 2525 (048 prefix from RoI).

- **Ashwood Trade Products**, Crown House, Home Gardens, Dartford, Kent DA1 1DZ, www.ashwood.biz, sales@ashwood.biz, (01332) 369000 (00 44 prefix from RoI).
- **Associated Craft Butchers of Ireland**, Research Office 1, Ashtown Food Research Centre, Teagasc, Ashtown, Dublin 15, www.craftbutchers.ie, (01) 868 2820.
- **Bakery Bits Ltd.**, 1 Orchard Units, Duchy Road, Honiton, Devon EX14 1YD, www.bakerybits.co.uk, enquiry@bakerybits.co.uk, (01404) 565656 (00 44 prefix from RoI).
- **Baldwin's Farmhouse Ice Cream**, Killeenagh, Knockanore, Co. Waterford, www.baldwinsicecream.com, thomas@baldwinsicecream.com, (086) 322 0932.
- **Ballymaloe Cookery School**, Shanagarry, Co. Cork, www.cookingisfun.ie, info@cookingisfun.ie, (021) 464 6785.
- **Bernie Quinn Duck Eggs**, Classaroe, Ballyhaunis, Co. Mayo, (086) 395 7059.
- **Bestbreadmachinereviews.com**, www.bestbreadmachinereviews.com.
- **Billy Bob's Pet & Country Superstore**, Unit 4, Cottage Hill, Loughrea, Co. Galway, www.billybobs.ie, (091) 847866.
- **Blas na hÉireann / National Irish Food Awards**, 10 Emlagh, Dingle, Co. Kerry, www.irishfoodawards.com, info@irishfoodawards.com, (087) 902 9329.
- **Bord Bia**, Clanwilliam Court, Lower Mount Street, Dublin 2, www.bordbia.ie / www.bordbiavantage.ie, (01) 668 5155.
- **Brandshapers Ltd.**, Ballytramon Business Park, Ardcavan, Castlebridge, Co. Wexford, www.brandshapers.ie, info@brandshapers.ie, (053) 917 7580.
- **Brennan Group**, Cloone, Co. Leitrim, www.brennan-group.com, info@brennan-group.com, (071) 963 6038.
- **Burren Smokehouse**, Kincora Road, Lisdoonvarna, Co. Clare, www.burrensmokehouse.ie, info@burrensmokehouse.ie, (065) 707 4432.
- *Buy & Sell*, www.buyandsell.ie.

- **C. van't Riet Dairy Technology BV**, Energieweg 20, 2421 LM Nieuwkoop, The Netherlands, www.rietdairy.nl/?lid=2, info@rietdairy.nl, (0172) 571304 (00 31 prefix from RoI).
- **CAFRE (College of Agriculture, Food & Rural Enterprise)**, Loughry College, Cookstown, Co. Tyrone BT80 9AA, www.cafre.ac.uk, enquiries@cafre.ac.uk, (028) 8676 8101 (048 prefix from RoI).
- **Cáis**, The Association of Irish Cheese-makers, www.irishcheese.ie.
- **Campden BRI**, Station Road, Chipping Campden, Gloucestershire GL55 6LD, www.campden.co.uk, info@campden.co.uk, (01366) 842000 (00 44 prefix from RoI).
- **Cannaboe Confectionery**, Willowfield Road, Ballinamore, Co. Leitrim, www.cacamilis.ie, info@cacamilis.ie, (071) 964 4778.
- **Carpigiani UK Ltd.**, Faculty House, 214 Holme Lacy Road, Hereford HR2 6BQ, www.carpigiani.co.uk, info@carpigiani.co.uk, (01432) 346018 (00 44 prefix from RoI).
- **Carrowholly Cheese**, Westport, Co. Mayo, carrowhollycheese@gmail.com, (087) 237 3536, contact Andrew Pelham Burn.
- **Castlehill Foods**, Carrowmore, Lacken, Killala, Co. Mayo, (096) 34111 / (087) 652 6065, contact Claire O'Connor
- **Cater Link**, Units 7-8, Bodmin Business Park, Launceston Road, Bodmin, Cornwall PL31 2RJ, www.caterlink.co.uk, sales@caterlink.co.uk, (01208) 78844 (00 44 prefix from RoI).
- **CaterPac @ Scallans Food Service Ltd.**, Whitemill Industrial Estate, Wexford, www.caterpac.ie, (053) 918 4745 / (087) 298 0558 (Sales).
- **CF Gaynor Ltd.**, Unit 19, Hub Logistics Park, Bracetown, Clonee, Dublin 15, www.cfgaynor.com, info@cfgaynor.com, (01) 825 2700.
- **Cherry Blossom Bakery**, Unit 7, Breaffy Business Park, Castlebar, Co. Mayo, www.cherryblossombakery.ie, cherryblossom@gmail.com, (094) 9038302.
- **Clonarn Clover**, www.clonarnclover.ie, roberto@clonarnclover.ie, (046) 924 2234.
- **Cloverhill Food Ingredients Ltd.**, Mountleader Industrial Estate, Millstreet, Co. Cork, www.cloverhill.ie, sales@cloverhill.ie, (029) 21844.

- **Coeliac Society of Ireland**, Carmichael House, 4 North Brunswick Street, Dublin 7, www.coeliac.ie, info@coeliac.ie, (01) 872 1471.
- **Connacht Gold**, Tubbercurry, Co. Sligo, www.connachtgold.ie, info@cgold.ie, (071) 918 6500.
- **Coopershill Venison**, Riverstown, Co. Sligo, www.coopershill.com /venison.html, venison@coopershill.com, (087) 792 8789.
- **Corleggy Cheeses**, Belturbet, Co. Cavan, www.corleggycheeses.com, contact Silke Croppe.
- **County and City Enterprise Boards**, www.enterpriseboards.ie.
- **County Dublin Beekeepers' Association**, www.dublinbees.org, info@dublinbees.org.
- **Crossgar Foodservice**, Farranfad Road, Seaforde, Downpatrick, BT30 8NH, Northern Ireland, online.crossgar.ie, sales@crossgar.ie, (028) 4481 1500 (048 prefix from RoI).
- **Cuinneog**, Balla, Castlebar, Co. Mayo, www.cuinneog.com, info@cuinneog.com, (094) 903 1425.
- **DairyCo**, Agriculture & Horticulture Development Board, Stoneleigh Park, Kenilworth, Warwickshire CV8 2TL, www.dairyco.org.uk, info@dairyco.ahdb.org.uk, (024) 7669 2051 (00 44 prefix from RoI).
- **Dairyglen**, Southern Cross Business Park, Bray, Co. Wicklow, www.dairyglen.ie, info@dairyglen.ie, (1890) 200052.
- **Department of Agriculture and Rural Development (NI)**, Dundonald House, Upper Newtownards Road, Ballymiscaw, Belfast BT4 3SB, www.dardni.gov.uk, dardhelpline@dardni.gov.uk, (028) 9052 4420 (048 prefix from RoI).
- **Department of Agriculture, Food and the Marine** (DAFM), Agriculture House, Kildare Street, Dublin 2, www.agriculture.gov.ie, info@agriculture.gov.ie, (01) 607 2000.
- **Done Deal**, www.donedeal.ie.
- **Dublin Institute of Technology**, School of Culinary Arts & Food Technology, Cathal Brugha Street, Dublin 1, www.dit.ie/culinaryartsandfoodtechnology/, Fabiola.Hand@dit.ie, contact Fabiola Hand.
- **Easy Equipment**, 66 Jersey Street, Manchester M4 6JQ, www.easyequipment.ie. sales@easyequipment.ie.

- **Enterprise Ireland**, Eastpoint Business Park, Dublin 3, www.enterprise-ireland.com, (01) 727 2000.

- **Environmental Health Officers' Association**, Heraghty House, 4 Carlton Terrace, Novara Avenue, Bray, Co. Wicklow, www.ehoa.ie, (01) 276 1211.

- **Environmental Protection Agency**, PO Box 3000, Johnstown Castle Estate, Wexford, www.epa.ie, (053) 916 0600.

- **Euro-Toques**, 11 Bridge Court, City Gate, St. Augustine's Street, Galway, www.euro-toques.ie, info@euro-toques.ie, (01) 677 9995.

- **Fáilte Ireland**, 85-95 Amiens Street, Dublin 1, www.failteireland.ie, customersupport@failteireland.ie, 1800 242473.

- **Featherbed Farm Luxury Ice Cream**, Featherbed Lane, Oylegate, Co. Wexford, www.featherbedfarm.ie, info@featherbedfarm.ie, (053) 917 7581.

- **Food Business Incubation Centre**, Loughry Campus, Cookstown, Co. Tyrone, www.cafre.ac.uk.

- **Food Flow Training**, Kinturk, Ballyheane, Co. Mayo, www.foodflow.ie, joe@foodflow.ie, (094) 903 0537.

- **Food Industry Training Unit**, College of Science, Engineering and Food Science, University College Cork, www.ucc.ie/fitu, m.mccarthybuckley@ucc.ie, (021) 490 3363.

- **Food Safety Authority of Ireland**, Abbey Court, Lower Abbey Street, Dublin 1, www.fsai.ie, info@fsai.ie, Advice line 1890 336677.

- **Food Standards Agency Northern Ireland**, 10c Clarendon Road, Belfast BT1 3BG, www.food.gov.uk/northern-ireland, (028) 9041 7700 (048 prefix from RoI).

- **Food Works**, www.foodworksireland.com, info@foodworksireland.com, (01) 668 5155.

- **Fullwood Ltd**, Grange Road, Ellesmere, Shropshire SY12 9DF, www.fullwood.com, sales@fullwood.com, (01691) 627391 (00 44 prefix from RoI).

- **Fuschia Brands**, West Cork Regional Branding Initiative, West Cork Technology Park, Clonakilty, Co. Cork, www.fuschiabrands,com, info@fuschiabrands.com, (023) 883 4035.

- **G&S Services Bakery Equipment Ltd.**, Unit 3, Hazelbank Mill, Gilford, Craigavon, Co. Armagh BT63 6DS, www.gandsbakeryequipment.co.uk, gandsservices@aol.com, (028) 4066 0492 (048 prefix from RoI).

- **Glastry Farm Ice Cream**, 43 Manse Road, Kirkubbin, Newtownards, Co. Down BT22 1DR, www.glastryfarm.com, (028) 4273 8671 (048 prefix from RoI).

- **Glenfin Free Range Duck Eggs**, Drumbenagh, Tydavnet, Co. Monaghan, www.glenfinfarm.ie, info@glenfinfarm.ie, (086) 171 4240.

- **Glenilen Farm**, Drimoleague, Co. Cork, www.glenilenfarm.com, val@glenilenfarm.com, (028) 31179.

- **Glenisk Organic Dairy**, Killeigh, Co. Offaly, www.glenisk.com, info@glenisk.com, (057) 934 4000.

- **Glyde Farm Produce**, Mansfieldstown, Castlebellingham, Co. Louth, glydefarm@eircom.net, (042) 937 2343.

- **Goat Nutrition Ltd.**, Units B&C, Smarsden Business Estate, Monks Hill, Smarsden, Ashford, Kent TN2 8QL, www.gnltd.co.uk, (01233) 770780 (00 44 prefix from RoI).

- **Good Food Ireland**, Ballykelly House, Drinagh, Co. Wexford, www.goodfoodireland.ie, info@goodfoodireland.ie, (053) 915 8693.

- **Great Taste Awards, Guild of Fine Food**, Guild House, 23b Kingsmead Business Park, Shaftesbury Road, Gillingham, SP8 5FB, UK, www.finefoodworld.co.uk, info@finefoodworld.co.uk, (01747) 825 200 (+44 prefix from RoI).

- **Grow It Yourself** (GIY), www.giyinternational.org, info@giyireland.com, (051) 302191.

- **Health Service Executive / Environmental Health Officers**, Oak House, Millennium Park, Naas, Co. Kildare, www.hse.ie/eng/services/list/1/environ/Contact.html, (045) 880400.

- **Horgan's Delicatessen Ltd.**, Mitchelstown Co. Cork, www.horgans.com, enquiries@horgans.com, (025) 41200.

- **Independent Irish Health Foods Ltd.**, Unit 12, Ballyvourney Industrial Estate, Ballyvourney, Co. Cork, www.iihealthfoods.com, (026) 65750.

- **Innovation Vouchers**, www.innovationvouchers.ie.

- **Institute of Marketecology**/Institut für Marketölogie, Weststrasse 51, CH-8570 Weinfelden, Switzerland, www.imo.ch, imo@imo.ch, (071) 626 0626 (00 41 prefix from RoI).

- **InterTradeIreland**, Old Gasworks Business Park, Kilmorey Street, Newry, Co. Down BT34 2DE, www.intertradeireland.com, info@intertradeireland.com, (028) 3083 4164 (048 prefix from RoI).

- **Irish Casing Company Ltd**, Spollanstown, Tullamore, Co. Offaly,www.irishcasings.com, info@irishcasings.com, (057) 932 1714.

- **Irish Farmers Association**, Irish Farm Centre, Bluebell, Dublin 12, www.ifa.ie, postmaster@ifa.ie, (01) 450 0266 – Alo Mohan, Chairman of National Poultry Committee, (087) 629 2456; Amii Cahill, Executive Secretary of National Poultry Committee, (01) 450 0266.

- **Irish Food Writers Guild**, www.irishfoodwritersguild.ie.

- **Irish Fowl**, www.irishfowl.com.

- **Irish Organic Farmers and Growers Association**, Unit 16A, Inish Carrig, Golden Island, Athlone, Co. Westmeath, www.iofga.org, info@iofga.org, (0906) 43680.

- **Irish Pasty People**, Crossmolina, Co. Mayo.

- **Irish Village Markets Ltd.,** 7 Windsor Place, Lanesville, Dun Laoire, Co. Dublin, www.irishvillagemarkets.ie, info@irishvillagemarkets.ie, (01) 284 1197.

- **Irish Yogurts**, Clonakilty, West Cork, www.irish-yogurts.ie, (023) 883 4745.

- **Irish-Poultry.com**, www.irish-poultry.com.

- **Jack & Eddie's Sausages**, Westport, Co. Mayo, www.jackandeddies.com, info@jackandeddies.com, (087) 234 9945.

- **James McGeough Butchers**, Camp Street, Oughterard, Co. Galway, www.connemarafinefoods.ie, connemarafinefoods@eircom.net, (091) 552 351.

- **James Whelan Butchers**, Oakville Shopping Centre, Clonmel, Co. Tipperary, www.jameswhelanbutchers.com, (052) 618 2477.

- **Jongia**, PO Box 284, 8901 BB Leeuwarden, The Netherlands, www.jongia.com, info@jongia.com, (0582) 139715 (00 31 prefix from RoI).

- **Kennedy Food Technology**, (086) 170 6939, contact Louise Kennedy.
- **Kilbeg Dairies**, Horath, Carlanstown, Kells, Co. Meath, www.kilbegdairies.ie, (046) 924 4687.
- **Killeen Farmhouse Cheese**, Loughanroe East, Ballyshrule, Ballinasloe, Co. Galway, www.killeencheese.ie, killeen.cheese@gmail.com, (0909) 741319.
- **Killowen Farm**, Courtnacuddy, Co. Wexford, www.killowen.ie, pauline@killowen.ie, (053) 924 4819.
- **Kitchen Incubators Kerry**, www.kitchenincubatorskerry.com, info@kitchenincubatorskerry.com, (087) 769 1136, contact Eileen McClure.
- **Knockanore Farmhouse Cheese Co. Ltd.**, Knockanore, Co. Waterford, www.knockanorecheese.com, eamon@knockanorecheese.com, (024) 97275.
- **Knockdrinna Farmhouse Cheese**, Stoneyford, Co. Kilkenny, www.knockdrinna.com, orders@knockdrinna.com, (056) 772 8446, contact Helen Finnegan.
- **LEADER / Rural Development Partnership Companies**, www.nrn.ie/leader-areas/.
- **Leatherhead Food Research**, Randalls Road, Leatherhead, Surrey KT22 7RY, www.leatherheadfood.com, help@leatherheadfood.com, (01372) 376761 (00 44 prefix from RoI).
- **Limerick Food Centre**, Raheen, Limerick.
- **Linnalla Ice Cream**, New Quay, The Burren, Co. Clare, www.linnallaicecream.ie, info@linnallaicecream.ie, (065) 707 8167.
- **Love Irish Food**, www.loveirishfood.ie.
- **M&K Meats Ltd.**, Unit 14 Block G, Greenogue Business Park, Rathcoole, Co. Dublin, www.mkmeats.eu, info@mkmeats.eu, (01) 458 7942.
- **MacEoin Poultry Supplies Ltd.**, Ballydavid, Co. Kerry, www.maceoinltd.com, (087) 207 7019.
- **Macs BBQ**, Unit 3A Rosevear Road Industrial Estate, Bugle, Cornwall, www.macsbbq.co.uk (01726) 851495 (00 44 prefix from RoI).

- **Make Icecream.com**, 29 Long Branch Avenue, Long Branch, NJ 07740, USA, www.makeicecream.com, sales@makeicecream.com.
- **Martin Food Equipment**, Dundalk, www.martinfoodequip.com, info@martinfoodequip.com, 1850 30 36 36.
- **McDonnell's Ltd.**, 19-20 Blackhall Street, Dublin 7, www.mcdonnells.ie, sales@mcdonnells.ie / info@mcdonnells.ie.
- **McGrath Bakery Services Ltd.**, 35a Donacloney Road, Dromore BT25 1JR, www.mbs-ltd.org, info@mbs-ltd.org, (028) 3888 1200 (048 prefix from RoI).
- **McNiffe's Bakery**, Aughnasheelin, Derrinkeher Roycroft, Co. Leitrim, www.mcniffesbakery.com, darren@mcniffesbakery.com, (071) 964 4625.
- **Molloy's Artisan Bakery / Honest**, Roscommon, www.molloysbakery.ie / www.honestbakery.ie, info@molloysbakery.ie, (0906) 625940.
- **Moorlands Cheesemakers Ltd.**, Lorien House, South Street, Castle Cary, Somerset BA7 7ES, www.cheesemaking.co.uk, info@cheesemaking.co.uk, (01963) 350634 (00 44 prefix from RoI).
- **Moy Valley Resources IRD**, Greenhills Enterprise Centre, Bunree Road, Ballina, Co. Mayo, www.moyvalley.ie, info@moyvalley.ie, (096) 70905.
- **Murphy's Ice Cream**, Strand Street, Dingle, Co. Kerry, www.murphysicecream.ie, (066) 915 2644.
- **Musgrave Food Services**, Musgrave Retailer Services, St. Margaret's Road, Ballymun, Dublin 11, foodservices.musgrave.ie, helpdesk2@musgrave.ie, (1890) 886 800.
- **National Dairy Council**, Innovation House, 3 Arkle Road, Sandyford Industrial Estate, Dublin 18, www.ndc.ie, info@ndc.ie, (01) 290 2451.
- **National Organic Training Skillnet** (NOTS), The Enterprise Centre, Hill Road, Drumshanbo, Co. Leitrim, www.nots.ie, info@nots.ie, (071) 964 0688 / (086) 172 8442.
- **Nisbets Next Day Catering Equipment**, North Link Business Park, Old Mallow Road, Cork, www.nisbets.ie, sales@nisbets.ie, (021) 494 6777.

- **North Tipperary Food Works**, Rearcross, Co. Tipperary, www.northtippfoodworks.ie, northtippfoodworks@gmail.com, (067) 33086.
- **Nutgrove Enterprise Park**, Nutgrove Way, Rathfarnham, Dublin 14, www.nutgrove-enterprisepark.ie, info@dlrceb.ie, (01) 494 8400.
- **Old McDonald's Farm & Feed Store**, Co. Carlow, www.oldmcdonald.ie, info@oldmcdonald.ie, (059) 917 9548 / (087) 279 7705.
- **Old Smokehouse Foods & Equipment**, Cookequip Ltd., Unit 4, Sumner Place, Addlestone, Surrey KT15 1QD, www.the-old-smokehouse.co.uk, sales@cookequip.co.uk, (01932) 841171 (00 44 prefix from RoI).
- **Omega Beef Direct**, Clashavaugha, Ballymacarbry, Clonmel, Co. Tipperary, www.omegabeefdirect.ie, info@omegabeefdirect.ie, (087) 273 5447.
- **Organic Trust Ltd.**, Vernon House, 2 Vernon Avenue, Clontarf, Dublin 3, www.organic-trust.org, organic@iol.ie, (01) 853 0271.
- **Paganini Ice Cream**, Kerlogue Industrial Centre, Rosslare Road, Wexford, www.paganini.ie, info@paganini.ie, (053) 914 7222.
- **Pallas Foods**, Newcastle West, Co. Limerick, www.pallasfoods.eu, info@pallasfoods.eu, (069) 20200.
- **Parkview Farm**, Tourlestrane, Co. Sligo, www.parkviewduckfarm.com, (087) 291 2664.
- **Pat O'Doherty**, Belmore Street, Enniskillen, Co. Fermanagh, www.blackbacon.com, p@blackbacon.com, (028) 6632 2152 (048 prefix from RoI).
- **Patents Office**, Government Buildings, Hebron Road, Kilkenny, www.patentsoffice.ie, patlib@patentsoffice.ie, (056) 772 0111.
- **Poultry Ireland**, www.poultry.ie.
- *Practical Poultry*, www.practicalpoultry.co.uk.
- **Quickcrop**, www.quickcrop.ie, info@quickcrop.ie, (01) 524 0884.
- **Rademaker BV**, Plantjinweg 23, PO Box 416, 4100 AK Culemborg, The Netherlands, www.rademaker.com, office@rademaker.com, (0345) 543 543 (00 31 prefix from RoI).

- **Rainbow Free Range Poultry**, Derrydonnell Mor, Athenry, Co. Galway, www.freerangepoultry.ie, tara@freerangepoultry.ie, (087) 919 9699.
- **Red's Sauces**, Westport, Co. Mayo, contact Redmond Cabot.
- **Robot Coupe (UK) Ltd.**, 2 Fleming Way, Isleworth TW7 6EU, www.robotcoupe.co.uk, sales@robotcoupe.co.uk, (0208) 232 1800 (00 44 prefix from RoI).
- **Rossmore Farmhouse Ice Cream**, Erril, Rathdowney, Co. Laois, www.rossmorefarm.ie, rossmoreicecream@gmail.com, (0505) 44292.
- **RSS Ltd.**, Hereford, Station Approach, Hereford, HR1 1BB, www.rsshereford.co.uk, sales@rsshereford.co.uk, (01432) 276777 (00 44 prefix from RoI).
- **Rural Development Partnerships / LEADER Companies**, www.nrn.ie.
- **SafeFood**, 7 Eastgate Avenue, Eastgate, Little Island, Cork, www.safefood.eu, (021) 230 4100.
- **Scobie & Junor (Dublin) Ltd.**, Unit D2, M7 Business Park, Newhall Interchange, Naas, Co. Kildare, www.scobiesdirect.com, info@scobiesdirect.com, (045) 899 177.
- **Scobie Bakery**, Scobie McIntosh Ltd, Oakwell Business Centre, Dark Lane, West Yorkshire WF14 9LW, www.scobiebakery.com, (01924) 432940 (00 44 prefix from RoI)
- **Sea Fisheries Protection Authority**, Park Road, Clogheen, Clonakilty, Co. Cork, www.sfpa.ie, sfpa_info@sfpa.ie, (023) 885 9300.
- **Servequip**, Suite 8, The Swift Centre, 41 Imperial Way, Croydon, Surrey CR0 4RL, www.servequip.co.uk, info@servequip.co.uk, (0208) 686 8855 (00 44 prefix from RoI).
- **Silver Pail Dairy**, Dublin Road, Fermoy, Co. Cork, www.silverpail.com, info@silverpail.com, (025) 31466.
- **Skillnets**, www.skillnets.ie.
- **Slow Food Ireland**, www.slowfoodireland.com.
- **Smallholding Courses**, www.smallholdingcourses.co.uk.
- **Smoky Jo's Cooking School**, Castle Court, Shap, Penrith, Cumbria CA10 3LG, www.smokyjos.co.uk, info@smokyjos.co.uk, (01931) 716638 (00 44 prefix from RoI).

- **Society of Dairy Technology**, Larnick Park, Higher Larrick, Trebullet, Launceston, Cornwall PL15 9QH, www.sdt.org, execdirector@sdt.org.
- **SPADE Enterprise Centre**, St. Paul's Church, North King Street, Dublin 7, (01) 617 4830, contact Susan Richardson, Centre Manager.
- **Specialist Cheesemakers Association**, 17 Clerkenwell Green, London EC1R 0DP, www.specialistcheesemakers.co.uk, info@specialistcheesemakers.co.uk, (0207) 608 1645 (00 44 prefix from RoI).
- **St. Angela's College**, Lough Gill, Sligo, stangelas.nuigalway.ie, admin@stangelas.nuigalway.ie, (071) 914 3580.
- **Stratton Sales & Service Inc.**, 1215 South Swaner Road, Salt Lake City, Utah 84104, USA, www.strattonsales.com, info@strattonsales.com, (801) 973 4041 (00 1 prefix from RoI).
- **Straw Chip**, Ballycullane, Athy, Co. Kildare, (059) 863 1623.
- **Sugarcraft.ie**, 64A Georges Street Upper, Dun Laoire, Co. Dublin, www.sugarcraft.ie, info@sugarcraft.ie, (01) 280 1870.
- **Taste 4 Success Skillnet**, PO Box 113, Rathowen, Co. Westmeath, www.taste4success.ie, info@taste4success.ie / training@taste4success.ie, (043) 668 5289.
- **TASTE Council**, www.tastecouncilofireland.com.
- **Teagasc (HQ)**, Oak Park, Carlow, www.teagasc.ie, (059) 917 0200.
- **Teagasc**, Ashtown, Dublin 15, www.teagasc.ie, (01) 805 9500.
- **Teagasc**, Moorepark Food Research Centre, Fermoy, www.teagasc.ie, niamh.obrien@teagasc.ie, (025) 42222, contact Niamh O'Brien.
- **Terenure Enterprise Centre**, Terenure, Dublin 6W, www.terenure-enterprise.ie, mhannan@terenure-enterprise.ie, (01) 490 3237.
- **The Cheese Hub**, Drumshambo, Co. Leitrim, www.thecheesehub.ie, info@thecheesehub.ie, (086) 172 8442 / (087) 273 7538.
- **The Cheese Web**, Eclectic Events Ltd., Old Woolman's House, Hastings Hill, Churchill, Oxfordshire OX7 6NA, www.thecheeseweb.com, cheese@thecheeseweb.com, (01608) 659325 (00 44 prefix from RoI).

- **The Federation of Irish Beekeepers' Associations**, c/o Michael Gleeson (Hon. Sec.), Ballinakill, Enfield, Co. Meath, www.irishbeekeeping.ie, mgglee@eircom.net, (046) 954 1433.
- **The Food Hub**, Carrick Road, Drumshanbo, Co. Leitrim, www.thefoodhub.com, info@thefoodhub.com, (071) 964 1848.
- **The Food Technology Centre**, St. Angela's College, Lough Gill, Sligo, www.thefoodtechnologycentre.ie, info@thefoodtechnologycentre, (071) 915 0734.
- **The Foods of Athenry**, Paul & Siobhan Lawless, Oldcastle, Kilconieron, Athenry, Co. Galway, www.foodsofathenry.ie, info@foodsofathenry.ie, (091) 848152.
- **The Ice Cream Alliance**, 3 Melbourne Court, off Island No. One, Derwent Parade, Pride Park, Derby DE24 8LZ, www.ice-cream.org, info@ice-cream.org, (01332) 203333 (00 44 prefix from RoI).
- **The Knead for Bread**, www.thekneadforbread.com.
- **The Organic Centre**, Rossinver, Co. Leitrim, www.theorganiccentre.ie, info@theorganiccentre.ie, (071) 985 4338.
- **Tipperary Organic Ice Cream**, c/o The Chocolate Garden, Tullow, Co. Carlow, www.tipperaryorganic.ie, info@tipperaryorganic.ie, (059) 648 1999.
- **Traditional Cheese Company**, Unit 241, Holly Road, Western Industrial Estate, Dublin 12, www.traditionalcheese.ie, info@traditionalcheese.ie, (01) 450 9494.
- **Údarás na Gaeltachta**, Na Forbacha, Co. na Gaillimhe, www.udaras.ie, eolas@udaras.ie, (091) 503100.
- **Ummera Smoked Products Ltd.**, Timoleague, Co. Cork, www.ummera.com, info@ummera.com, (023) 884 6644.
- **Úna's Pies**, Ballincollig. Co. Cork, www.unaspies.ie.
- **Valentia Island Farmhouse Dairy**, Valentia, Co. Kerry, www.valentiadairy.com, valentiaicecream@eircom.net, (066) 947 6864.
- **Westport Grove Jams and Chutneys**, Westport, Co. Mayo, absfcasey@eircom.net, (087) 237 2479, contact Sean Casey.
- **Wholefoods Wholesale Ltd.**, www.wholefoods.ie.

ABOUT THE AUTHOR

Oonagh Monahan has a Bachelor of Science, a Graduate Diploma in Food Science & Technology and a Master of Engineering Science degree (from the Department of Agricultural & Food Engineering at University College Dublin). For her Master's research, Oonagh won a scholarship sponsored by H.J. Heinz. In addition, Oonagh has a Diploma in Training & Education from NUI Galway and has qualifications in Marketing Management. Her experience in the food sector includes roles as Food Technologist and Quality Control Manager with Manor Bakeries Ltd in England (Mr. Kipling cakes) and Quality Assurance Manager with Kerry Foods plc (Grove Turkeys). She subsequently moved to a position as General Manager of the Food Technology Centre in St. Angela's College, Sligo, where she was responsible for business development of the centre and developing food product development and innovation projects with food producers.

In January 2008, Oonagh set up Alpha Omega Consultants, where she uses her extensive experience to devise, deliver, facilitate and manage support programmes for the small food sector. Oonagh continues to work occasionally as a food product development lecturer at St. Angela's College, working on practical product development with Home Economics students and she also lectures in EU and Irish Food Legislation.

She is a food business development mentor with Enterprise Ireland, South West Mayo Development, Mayo North East Partnership, Sligo Leader Partnership Company and the Sligo, Mayo, Leitrim, Roscommon, Cavan and Westmeath County Enterprise Boards for new food start-up companies. She is a Fellow of the Institute of Food Science & Technology (UK), a Fellow of the Institute of Food Science & Technology of Ireland, a Member of the Institute of Management Consultants and Advisors (IMCA) and a Certified Management Consultant (CMC). Oonagh was a founder of the Harvest Feast Food Festival In Co. Leitrim and is also involved with the So Sligo Food Festival. Oonagh has the very difficult job of acting as an assessor for a number of restaurant awards competitions – it's not easy!

Oonagh is a keen home cook and has attended the Ballymaloe, Source Sligo and Belle Isle Cookery Schools. She has a real interest in the preparation, presentation and service of good food, using quality ingredients, local and seasonal where possible, whether fine dining or gastro pub, food stall or at home. She has travelled in the UK, USA, France, Holland, Spain, Italy, Malaysia, Newfoundland, Singapore and Croatia in recent years, as well as extensive travelling within the island of Ireland. Places to eat on the road or on holiday are a very important consideration!

Oonagh's blog **oonagheats.com** tries to capture all her experiences and opinions, the good and the bad, at home and abroad.

OAK TREE PRESS

Oak Tree Press develops and delivers information, advice and resources for entrepreneurs and managers. It is Ireland's leading business book publisher, with an unrivalled reputation for quality titles across business, management, HR, law, marketing and enterprise topics. NuBooks is its recently-launched imprint, publishing short, focused ebooks for busy entrepreneurs and managers.

In addition, through its founder and managing director, Brian O'Kane, Oak Tree Press occupies a unique position in start-up and small business support in Ireland through its standard-setting titles, as well as training courses, mentoring and advisory services.

Oak Tree Press is comfortable across a range of communication media – print, web and training, focusing always on the effective communication of business information.

Oak Tree Press, 19 Rutland Street, Cork, Ireland.
T: + 353 21 4313855 F: + 353 21 4313496.

E: info@oaktreepress.com W: www.oaktreepress.com.

Lightning Source UK Ltd.
Milton Keynes UK
UKOW05f1355300417

300190UK00001B/29/P